D1616561

Alissa
Grade 6 2011

B.C. Science PROBE 5

Authors

Susan Doyle
Curriculum Writer and Author
Writing Instructor, University of Victoria

Jean Bowman
Saanich School District (#63), B.C.

Susan Martin
Delta School District (#37), B.C.

Heather Stannard
Cowichan Valley School District (#79), B.C.

Program Consultant

Arnold Toutant
Educational Consultant,
A. Toutant Consulting Group Ltd.

THOMSON
NELSON

Australia   Canada   Mexico   Singapore   Spain   United Kingdom   United States

THOMSON

NELSON

B.C. Science Probe 5

Authors
Susan Doyle
Jean Bowman
Susan Martin
Heather Stannard

Program Consultant
Arnold Toutant

Director of Publishing:
Beverley Buxton

General Manager, Mathematics, Science, & Technology:
Lenore Brooks

Publisher, Science:
John Yip-Chuck

Executive Managing Editor, Special Projects:
Cheryl Turner

Managing Editor, Science:
Lois Beauchamp

Program Manager:
Lee Geller

Project Editor:
Lee Ensor

Developmental Editor:
Janis Barr

Editorial Assistants:
Jacquie Busby,
Christina D'Alimonte

Executive Managing Editor, Production:
Nicola Balfour

Senior Production Editor:
Deborah Lonergan

Copy Editor:
Paula Pettitt-Townsend

Proofreader:
Susan McNish

Indexer:
Noeline Bridge

Senior Production Coordinator:
Sharon Latta Paterson

Design Director:
Ken Phipps

Text Design:
Kyle Gell Design

Art Management:
Kathy Karakasidis, Allan Moon

Composition Team:
Kyle Gell Design, Allan Moon

Cover Design:
Peter Papayanakis

Cover Image:
© Gunter Marx Photography/Corbis

Illustrators:
Greg Banning
Barry Cohen
Steven Corrigan
Deborah Crowle
Margo Davies LeClair
Kathy Karakasidis
Dave Mazierski
Dave McKay
Allan Moon
Rolin Graphics
Bart Vallecoccia
Dave Whamond

Photo Research and Permissions:
Mary Rose MacLachlan

Printer:
Transcontinental Printing Inc.

ISBN: 0-17-628280-7

Reviewers

Contents

Chapter 3

UNIT B: THE HUMAN BODY

Chapter 6

Chapter 7

UNIT C: EARTH'S RESOURCES

Expanding the World of Science

What do scientists do?

If you had to answer this question, what would you say?

The dictionary says that a scientist is a person with expert knowledge of a science. Science is knowledge that is learned through exploration, observation, and doing experiments. For example, we know that some resources are renewable while other resources cannot be renewed. This knowledge came from scientists carefully observing living and non-living things.

Scientists are not the only people who observe living and non-living things. People who have lived for a very long time in one place get to know the nature of the place very well. Different groups of Aboriginal peoples have lived in parts of what is now known as British Columbia for many generations. Some Aboriginal peoples have detailed knowledge about the animals, the plants, the weather, and the land close to their homes. They have learned how all the different parts of nature work together and affect each other. This information is a very important part of science.

This information, known as **Indigenous Knowledge** (IK) or Traditional Ecological Knowledge (TEK), was passed to the next generation through stories and songs. Now this information is being written down because it can help all people learn better ways to live in our world.

In British Columbia, as in other places around the world, more and more scientists are asking to work with and learn from Aboriginal peoples and their communities. It is important to Aboriginal peoples that their ways are respected and valued by others. We can all learn from the information that Aboriginal peoples have to share.

Mary-Anne Smirle
Métis Nation
L'Hirondelle clan

Unit A

Forces and Machines

Chapter 1 Forces around us affect the movement of objects.

Chapter 2 Machines use forces to do work.

Chapter 3 We use simple and compound machines to do work for us.

NEL

Preview

A roller coaster takes you on a thrilling ride as it rushes down the track. You feel your body being pushed and pulled as the car moves through fast turns. You feel yourself being lifted into the air on steep drops. You find yourself turned upside down on loops. Then, as you speed down the track, you're pushed back, flat against your seat. What is pushing and pulling you? What is holding you in your seat when you're upside down?

In this unit, you will learn about the forces that push and pull on you. You will learn how these forces affect the way everything moves. You will discover how machines use these forces to do amazing things. You will also discover how we use machines to make our daily life in British Columbia easier and more comfortable.

Make a Roller Coaster

Skills Focus: creating models, predicting, observing

1. Use strips of heavy paper or cardboard to build a flexible track that is about 3 m long. Tape the end of the track to the back of your chair to create your first hill.

2. Build a second hill using the seat of another chair, books, or other objects in the classroom. Place the track over the hill.

3. Release a marble from the top of the first hill to test your roller coaster. Does the marble travel to the end of the track?

4. Experiment with the height of the second hill. How high can you make this hill and still have the marble travel to the end of the track?

◀ Machines, like roller coasters, use forces to keep the coaster on the track in the twists and turns.

Forces around us affect the movement of objects.

➡ **Key Ideas**

▸ A force is a push or pull that moves an object or holds it in place.

▸ Forces can be measured with a spring scale.

▸ Friction is a force that slows or stops movement.

▸ Surface texture, slope, and load affect the amount of force needed to make an object move.

▸ Forces can be combined to affect the way things move.

Skateboarders can really move! Some skateboarders look like they're flying through the air as they twist and turn. Then they land on the ground and come to a sudden stop. How can they change direction in a split second? How can they start and stop moving so quickly? Forces help skateboarders move, change direction, and stop.

In this chapter, you will learn about the ways that forces affect how things move. You will learn that forces can be used to start and stop motion and to change an object's speed and direction. You will also learn that other things affect the amount of force needed to make an object move.

What Makes Things Move?

◀ You use a pushing force when you kick a soccer ball.

⚡ Learning Tip

Important vocabulary words are highlighted. Make sure you understand what these words mean.

Have you ever played soccer? If you have, then you know that you have to use force to make the soccer ball go where you want it to go. A **force** is a push or a pull on an object. When you kick a soccer ball, you are pushing the ball in the direction you want it to go. When a goalie stops the ball, the goalie is pulling the ball in a different direction to stop it from going into the net.

▲ When you pull an object in the direction you want it to go, you are using force.

Forces are all around you. They affect everyone and everything in different ways. You can see the effects of some forces, like the wind, the force of your foot kicking a soccer ball, or the pull or push of a magnet. There are also forces that are invisible, like the force of gravity [GRAV-uh-tee] pulling you to the ground.

Try This

Observe a Bouncing Ball

Skills Focus: observing, measuring

1. Drop a ball from a height of 1 m. Record how high the ball bounces.

2. How can you change the force you use on the ball to make the ball bounce higher or lower? Try it and see.

3. How did changing the force change the height that the ball bounced?

In the Try This activity, forces made the ball move. When you dropped the ball, the force of gravity pulled it to the ground. When you changed the force you used on the ball, the motion changed. For instance, when you increased the force you used on the ball, the ball bounced higher. The force you use affects how an object moves.

Try This

Observe How a Ball Moves

Skills Focus: predicting, observing, measuring

1. Roll the ball toward another student in your group. Change the force you use on the ball to make the ball roll faster. Now, change the force you use on the ball to make it roll slower.

2. Roll the ball around in the circle formed by your legs. Use force to make the ball change direction.

3. How can you use force to change the speed and direction of the ball?

You were able to control the speed and direction that the ball moved by controlling how you used force. When the amount of force used on an object changes, the motion of the object changes. For instance, when you changed the amount of force you used, the speed of the ball changed. When you changed the direction of the force, the direction of the ball changed. You were able to stop the ball by using force.

Forces affect the motion of objects around us every day. Some forces make things move. Other forces slow things down, stop them, or hold them in place.

⇨ Check Your Understanding

1. What is a force?

2. Think about riding a bike or going skateboarding. Choose one of these activities and describe, in words or pictures, how force is used to
   - start and stop moving
   - change speed
   - change direction

② Measuring Forces

You can measure forces using a spring scale. A spring scale measures force in a unit called newtons [NOO-tuhnz]. The symbol for newtons is N.

Weight [WAYT] is a measure of the force of gravity on an object. When you hang an object from the hook on a spring scale, the downward force of gravity stretches the spring. The scale shows the strength of the force of gravity in newtons.

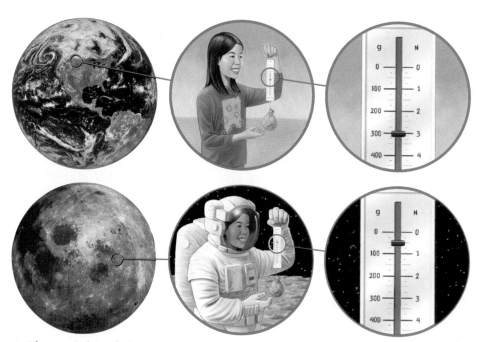

▲ The weight of the marbles is 3.0 N on Earth, but only 0.5 N on the Moon.

The force of gravity is different depending on where you are. The force of gravity on Earth is about six times as great as the force of gravity on the Moon. There are even differences in the force of gravity at different places on Earth. The farther you are away from the centre of Earth, the less gravity is pulling on you.

Measure Force

Skills Focus: predicting, observing, measuring

1. Using string, tie a 500 mL bottle with 400 mL of water in it to a spring scale. Pull the bottle up so that it is hanging from the spring scale. Hold it still to measure the force of gravity.

2. Predict how the amount of force would change if you measured the force acting on two identical bottles. Tie another bottle to the spring scale, and pull up both bottles. Read the measurement on the spring scale.

3. Work with a partner. Attach two spring scales to one bottle. Pull equally to raise the bottle. Read the spring scales when the bottle is still. How does the amount of force change when two people lift the bottle?

4. Predict how the amount of force would change if three or four people lifted the bottle. Try this to check your prediction.

⇨ Learning Tip

To read the measurement on a spring scale correctly, make sure that you look at the scale at eye level.

⇨ Check Your Understanding

1. What tool can you use to measure force?
2. Would you expect to get the same results in the Try This activity if you did it on the Moon? Explain your answer.

3 Friction

⇨ Learning Tip

Check your understanding of friction by finding examples from your own life. When have you noticed friction slow something down or make something hard to move?

Try This

Observe Friction

Skills Focus: observing, inferring

1. Rub your hands together for one minute. What do you feel? What do you hear?

2. Put some liquid soap on your hands, and rub them again. What differences do you notice from step 1?

3. Cover your desk with a piece of newspaper. Rub two small pieces of sandpaper together. What do you feel? What do you hear? Is there anything on the newspaper?

Friction [FRIK-shun] is a force that resists movement. Friction slows down moving objects and makes objects that are not moving hard to move. Friction can create noise and heat. When you did the Try This activity, you experienced friction. When you rubbed your hands together, you heard the friction and felt your hands get warm. Friction can also cause surfaces to wear away, as you saw when you rubbed together two pieces of sandpaper.

The way your running shoes keep you from sliding across a wood or tiled floor is an example of friction. Basketball players need friction between their shoes and the floor, so they can control how they move.

◄ The friction between a basketball player's shoes and the floor stops the basketball player from sliding forward.

When two things come in contact with each other, there is friction. Imagine pushing a box along a floor. The force of friction acting on the box occurs between the surface of the floor and the side of the box sliding along the floor.

⇨ **Learning Tip**

Read the first paragraph on this page and examine the diagram and the caption below it. Then use your own words to explain the diagram to a partner.

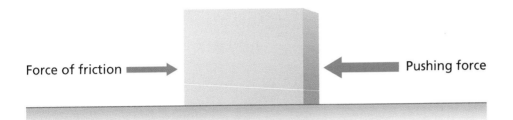

Force of friction ➡   ⬅ Pushing force

▲ Friction occurs between the bottom of the box and the floor.

Friction and Surface Texture

Friction occurs because surfaces are not perfectly smooth. Even ice, which looks perfectly smooth, actually has a bumpy, uneven surface.

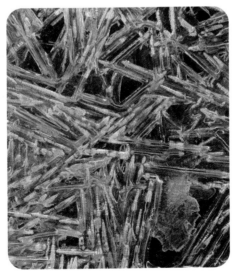

▲ Ice may look smooth, but, when it is magnified 20 times, you can see its rough surface.

The amount of friction between two objects depends on what the objects are made from. Different objects feel different when you touch them. The way that an object feels is called its **surface texture.** Surfaces can be rough, smooth, or slippery. How would you describe the surface texture of sandpaper, a mirror, and liquid soap?

Surface texture affects the amount of friction between two surfaces. The rougher the surfaces, the more friction there is between the objects. If you move an object over a rough surface, such as a bumpy sidewalk, you will have to use more force than if you move the same object over a smoother surface, such as ice.

▶ Movement is easy on a smooth surface, like ice, because there is less friction to slow things down.

The Advantages and Disadvantages of Friction

Friction is helpful to us in many ways. Without friction, you would not be able to walk. Your feet would slip out from under you! It is the friction between the surface of your shoes and the ground that allows you to walk. Friction also lets you slow down or stop moving. Bicycles need the friction between their brakes and their wheels, and between their wheels and the road, to slow them down.

▶ The friction between two surfaces slows movement. It makes it possible for us to slow down and stop.

12

Sometimes friction can be a disadvantage. Friction slows down objects and makes them harder to move. When you are skating or going down a waterslide, you want to go fast. It is friction that slows you down.

If you are snowboarding, friction slows you down as you travel over the snow. To go faster, you have to spread wax over the bottom surface of the snowboard to reduce friction. However, you also need friction when you are snowboarding. The edges of the snowboard are shaped to make use of friction. The edges are sharp so that you can control your movement when turning and stop when you need to.

▲ The water on a waterslide reduces friction so you can go faster.

◄ Snowboarders want less friction so they can go fast, but they also need friction to control their speed and direction.

⇨ Check Your Understanding

1. What is friction? How does friction change the way things move?
2. Name three things that can happen when two surfaces rub together.
3. How does surface texture affect the amount of friction between objects?
4. Draw two pictures. In one picture, show an activity where friction is an advantage. In the other picture, show an activity where friction is a disadvantage. Write one sentence for each picture to explain your ideas.

4 Design Your Own Experiment

○ SKILLS MENU

◉ Questioning	◉ Measuring
◉ Predicting	○ Classifying
◉ Designing Experiments	○ Inferring
◉ Fair Testing	◉ Interpreting Data
◉ Observing	◉ Communicating

⇨ **Learning Tip**

Before you begin this experiment, review Design Your Own Experiment in the Skills Handbook.

How Does Surface Texture Affect Force?

Design an experiment to find out how much force is needed to move a block across a surface covered with three different textures.

Question

Write a question about how surface texture affects the force that is required to move an object. For example, your question could be "Which surface will require the most force to move a block 1 m: sandpaper, carpet, or cardboard?"

Prediction

Look carefully at each surface. Rub your hand over each surface. Use your observations to predict which surface will need the greatest amount of force to move the block.

Materials

Decide what materials you will need to conduct your experiment. Check with your teacher to make sure that these materials are safe for you to use.

○ Procedure

- Design a procedure to test your prediction. Your procedure is a step-by-step description of how you will conduct your experiment. It must be clear enough for someone else to follow and do the same experiment. You will need to conduct more than one trial for each surface you test.
- Hand in your procedure, including any safety precautions, to your teacher for approval.

Data and Observations

Create a data table to record your observations. Record your observations as you carry out your experiment.

Interpret Data and Observations

1. Which surface required the greatest amount of force to move the block?

2. Which surface required the least amount of force to move the block?

3. How did the surface texture affect the amount of force needed to move the block?

4. Look back at your prediction. Did your results fully support, partly support, or not support your prediction? Write a conclusion for your experiment.

Apply and Extend

1. Think about the surface textures you tested. Which surface would be best for inline skating? Which surface would be best to make sure you don't slip?

2. Repeat this experiment, but move the block up a ramp and keep the surface texture the same. Try a few different ramp heights. What effect does changing the height of the ramp have on the force needed to move the block up the ramp?

⇨ Check Your Understanding

1. What variable did you change in your experiment?
2. What variable did you measure?
3. What variables did you keep the same?
4. Was your experiment a fair test? How do you know?

What Affects the Amount of Force Needed to Move an Object?

 Try This

Predict What Affects Force

Skills Focus: predicting, observing, measuring, inferring

1. Place an object in the box. Use a spring scale to measure the amount of force needed to pull the box across the floor or a table.

2. What could you do that would increase the amount of force needed to move the box? What could you do that would decrease the amount of force needed to move the box? Copy the table on the right into your notebook. Write your predictions in your table.

3. Test the predictions you wrote in your table. Use a spring scale to measure the force.

What Affects Force

Prediction	Was your prediction correct?
I would need to use more force if...	
I would need to use less force if...	

Forces affect the way things move. You need forces to start and stop the motion of an object. There are things that affect the amount of force you need to make an object move. For example, surface texture, slope [SLOHP], and load all affect the amount of force you need to make an object move.

Surface Texture

You have learned that surface texture affects the amount of friction between two surfaces. The more friction there is between two surfaces, the more force you need to make an object move.

Slope

Slope affects the amount of force needed to make an object move. Slope is a change in height between two points. When a surface is sloped, it is on an angle. For example, the roofs of many houses are sloped. A sloped surface is also called a **ramp.**

When slope changes, the amount of force needed to move an object also changes. Moving an object up a ramp requires more force than moving an object across a flat surface. If you increase the slope of a ramp, the amount of force you need to move an object up the ramp also increases.

▲ The rough surface texture of the sandpaper creates a lot of friction between the sandpaper and the wood.

⇨ **Learning Tip**

Look at the section title and the headings on this page and the next page. When you have finished reading this section, check your understanding by answering the question in the section title.

▲ If you ride a bike up the slope of a hill, you need to use a lot of force.

Moving an object down a ramp requires less force than moving an object across a flat surface. If you increase the slope of a ramp, the amount of force you need to move an object down the ramp decreases.

▲ If you ride down a hill, you need to use less force.

Load

Load affects the amount of force needed to make an object move. **Load** is the weight of the object you are trying to move. The larger the load is, the more force you need to move it. For example, you need more force to lift a backpack with four textbooks in it than a backpack with one textbook in it.

▲ You need more force to lift a backpack when you increase the load of the backpack.

1. Look at each pair of pictures. What is affecting the amount of force needed to move? Which student in each pair of pictures would be able to use the least amount of force?

A   B

A   B

A   B

⑥ Conduct an Investigation

⚙ SKILLS MENU

○ Questioning	● Measuring
● Predicting	○ Classifying
○ Designing Experiments	○ Inferring
● Fair Testing	● Interpreting Data
● Observing	● Communicating

⟳ Learning Tip

To make sure that your test is fair, you must use the same materials and release the cans in the same way in all the trials. You must follow exactly the same steps in all the trials. These steps are your procedure. Before you begin this investigation, review Conduct an Investigation in the Skills Handbook.

textbooks

board

empty can

masking tape

measuring tape

full can

How Do Slope and Load Affect How Far a Can Rolls?

You have learned that many things affect how an object moves. In this investigation, you will conduct a fair test to find out how load and the slope of a ramp affect how far an object travels when it is rolled down the ramp.

Questions

- How does increasing the load affect how far a can rolls?
- How does increasing the slope affect how far a can rolls?

Prediction

Write your predictions before you begin your investigation.
- Which do you think will travel farther, an empty can or a full can? Explain why.
- Which do you think will travel farther, a full can rolled down a two-book slope or a full can rolled down a four-book slope? Explain why.

Materials

- 4 textbooks
- board, 150 cm × 30 cm
- empty can

- masking tape
- measuring tape
- full can

In your notebook, make a table like the one below.

Data Table for Investigation 1.6		Distance Travelled		
		Trial 1	Trial 2	Trial 3
Testing the load	two-book slope with empty can			
	two-book slope with full can			
Testing the slope	two-book slope with full can			
	four-book slope with full can			

Testing the Load

Step 1 Build a ramp by placing two books under one end of the board. Be sure to leave a lot of space for the cans to roll.

Step 2 Release the empty can from the top of the ramp. Use a piece of masking tape to mark the place where the can stops rolling.

Step 3 Measure the distance the empty can travelled, from the end of the ramp to where it stopped rolling. Record the distance in your table under Trial 1.

Step 4 Repeat steps 2 and 3 two more times. Record the distances in your table under Trial 2 and Trial 3.

Step 5 Release the full can from the top of the ramp. Use a piece of masking tape to mark the place where the can stops rolling.

Step 6 Measure the distance the full can travelled, from the end of the ramp to where it stopped rolling. Record the distance in your table under Trial 1.

Step 7 Repeat steps 5 and 6 two more times, and record the distances in your table under Trial 2 and Trial 3.

Testing the Slope

Step 1 In steps 5 to 7 in Testing the Load, you tested how far a full can travels on a two-book slope. Copy your results for these trials into the next row of your table.

Step 2 Increase the slope of the ramp by adding two more books to it.

Step 3 Release the full can from the top of the ramp. Use a piece of masking tape to mark the place where the can stops rolling.

Step 4 Measure the distance the can travelled, from the end of the ramp to where it stopped rolling. Record the distance in your table under Trial 1.

Step 5 Repeat steps 3 and 4 two more times. Record the distances in your table under Trial 2 and Trial 3.

Interpret Data and Observations

1. In the Testing the Load section, which can travelled farther, the empty can or the full can? How does load affect the distance that an object moves?

2. Which slope made the can travel farther, the two-book slope or the four-book slope? How does the slope of a ramp affect the distance that an object moves?

3. Were your predictions correct?

Apply and Extend

1. How could roller-coaster designers use the information from this investigation?

2. Do you think you would get the same results if you used different surfaces for the ramp when testing the full can and the empty can on the two-book slope? Conduct an investigation to test your prediction.

⇨ Check Your Understanding

1. What variables were the same in all trials in the load test? What variables were the same in all trials in the slope test?

2. What other variables could have affected your results?

3. Why were you asked to do more than one trial for each test?

4. Do you think your tests were fair? Explain your thinking.

7 Combining Forces

Most objects have more than one force acting on them at the same time. When forces combine, they affect the way that an object moves.

▲ When you fly a kite, gravity, the wind, and the pull of the string affect how high and in what direction the kite flies.

Pushing force of desk upward

Pulling force of gravity downward

▲ When the forces are equal, the pencil will not move.

Balanced Forces

Consider a pencil sitting on your desk. What forces are acting on it? There is the downward pull of gravity and the upward push of your desk. When two forces of equal strength act in opposite directions, they are called **balanced forces.** As long as the two forces acting on the pencil remain balanced, the pencil will not move.

When the forces on an object are balanced, the object is said to be in **equilibrium** [EE-kwuh-LIHB-ree-um]. When an object is in equilibrium, there is no change in the motion of the object.

1. Work with a partner. Stand back to back, leaning against each other. Slowly move your feet away from your partner until they are about 1 m apart. Continue pushing against each other, trying to remain balanced and motionless. Think about the way that you and your partner are using force to remain balanced.

2. Slowly bend your knees. How have you adjusted the amount of force you are using to remain balanced and motionless?

3. How would your movement change if one person used more force than the other?

Unbalanced Forces

Think back to the pencil on your desk. To change the motion of the pencil, one of the forces has to be greater than the other, or a new force has to be added. For example, if you add a force by gently pushing the pencil with your finger, the pencil will move in the direction of the new force you added.

➡ Learning Tip

To check your understanding of balanced and unbalanced forces, explain them to a partner. Use a different example than the pencil on a desk.

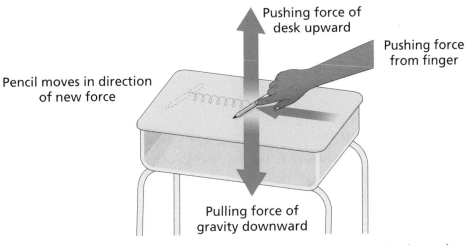

Pushing force of desk upward

Pushing force from finger

Pencil moves in direction of new force

Pulling force of gravity downward

▲ When a new force is added, the combined forces are unbalanced and there is a change in the motion of the pencil.

Unbalanced forces happen when one of the forces acting on an object is greater than another force acting in the opposite direction. When you pushed the pencil with your finger, the forces acting on the pencil became unbalanced. The pencil moved because there was no other force to balance the force you applied with your finger. The pencil moved in the direction of the greater force.

When the forces acting on an object are unbalanced, the motion of the object usually changes. The pencil moved because the forces acting on it were unbalanced. If you know the size and direction of all the forces acting on an object, you can predict how an object may move.

⇨ Learning Tip

Check your understanding of what you have just read by trying to answer the questions under the photo. Then read the last paragraph to see if your answers were correct.

▲ What forces are acting on this toboggan to keep it sitting at the top of the hill? How could the forces change? What would happen if they did?

Think about the forces acting on a toboggan when it is sitting at the top of a hill. There is the downward force of gravity and the upward force of the ground. As long as these forces are equal, the movement of the toboggan will not change. The toboggan is in equilibrium. If you add another force, such as the force of using your arms to push you forward, the toboggan will move forward because the forces are no longer balanced.

1. Write two or three sentences to explain what will happen when one student joins one of the sides. Use the words equilibrium, balanced, and unbalanced in your sentences.

2. Tugboats are used to push or pull barges that are loaded with heavy containers. Draw a sketch with arrows to show how tugboats and a barge will move in each of the following situations:
   - Two identical tugboats are pulling a barge upstream together.
   - Two identical tugboats are pulling a barge in opposite directions.
   - One tugboat is more powerful than the other tugboat, and they are pulling in opposite directions.

Barge

Tugboat

Chapter **1**

Chapter Review

Forces around us affect the movement of objects.

Key Idea: A force is a push or pull that moves an object or holds it in place.

Vocabulary
force p. 5

Key Idea: Forces can be measured with a spring scale.

Vocabulary
weight p. 8

Key Idea: Friction is a force that slows or stops movement.

Vocabulary
friction p. 10
surface texture
  p. 11

Key Idea: Surface texture, slope, and load affect the amount of force needed to make an object move.

surface texture

slope

load

Vocabulary
ramp p. 17
load p. 18

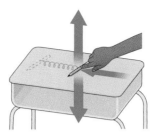

Key Idea: Forces can be combined to affect the way things move.

Vocabulary
balanced forces p. 24
equilibrium p. 24
unbalanced forces p. 26

Review Key Ideas and Vocabulary

Use the vocabulary words in your answers to the questions.

1. What are forces? How do forces affect the way that things move?

2. How can you measure the amount of force that is needed to pull a toy car toward you?

3. Explain how putting sand on an icy road can help prevent cars from sliding.

4. Use drawings and words to explain how load, slope, and surface texture can affect the way the bobsled moves.

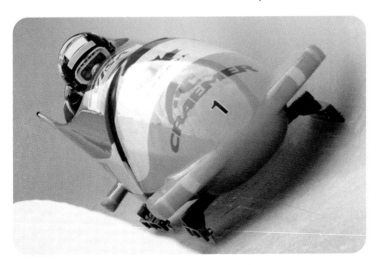

5. Use the words balanced forces and unbalanced forces to explain why the ball is not moving. What could change the motion of the ball?

Design and Build a Car

Looking Back

You have learned

- that forces can be measured using a spring scale
- that friction, load, surface texture, and slope affect the way that things move
- that forces can combine to affect the way that things move

In this activity, you will work in a group to design and build a car that travels the greatest distance off the end of a ramp.

Demonstrate Your Learning

Design and Build a Car

1. Work with a group to design a car that you think will travel as far as possible off the end of a ramp. Think back to what you have learned about load. How can you use load to your advantage? Think back to what you have learned about friction and surface texture.

2. Draw and label a design for a car. Show your design to your teacher. Once you have your teacher's approval, build your car.

3. In your notebook, make a table like the one below.

	Weight of Car (N)	Distance Travelled	Changes to Car	
Trial 1				
Trial 2				
Trial 3				

4. Use a spring scale to weigh your car. Record the weight.

Test and Evaluate

1. Your teacher will provide you with a ramp.

2. Release your car from the top of the ramp. Use a piece of masking tape to mark the place where the car stops rolling.

3. Measure the distance your car travelled, from the end of the ramp to where it stopped rolling. Record the distance.

4. Modify the design of your car. In your table, describe the change(s) you made. Measure the weight of your car, and repeat steps 2 and 3.

5. Complete step 4 at least one more time.

Communicate

1. Demonstrate your best design to the class. Explain how you increased the distance your car travelled.

⇨ Assessment Checklist

DESIGN AND BUILD A CAR

As you build and test your car, make sure that you show you are able to

✔ use a spring scale correctly
✔ recognize the effects of friction and load
✔ accurately record your observations
✔ use appropriate scientific words
✔ communicate clearly
✔ work cooperatively with other students

chapter 2

Machines use forces to do work.

Can you imagine trying to chop wood without an axe? How would you do it? What if you had to move a load of rocks or soil without a wheelbarrow? What if you had to lift a car to change a tire without a jack? How would you open a door without a doorknob? All of these jobs would be much more difficult to do without machines [muh-SHEENZ].

In this chapter, you will discover how machines make use of forces to do work. You will learn about six simple machines: the lever, the wheel and axle [AK-suhl], the pulley, the inclined plane, the wedge [WEJ], and the screw. You will discover the many ways we use simple machines to make our work easier.

Machines Make Work Easier

Has your teacher ever asked you to get to work? Does it seem like work when you ride a bicycle up a hill? We use the word "work" to mean different things. When scientists use the word "work," they mean something very specific.

In science, you are doing **work** when you use force to make something move. For example, you are doing work when you roll a large ball of snow to make a snow person. You are applying force to an object that causes that object to move. The amount of work you do depends on the amount of force you use and the distance the object moves.

Force applied

Distance moved

▲ When you roll a ball of snow to make a snow person, you are doing work.

Machines

A machine makes work easier to do. A pencil sharpener is a machine that helps you sharpen a pencil more easily than you could without using it. Using a machine does not usually mean that you do less work. It usually means that you do the work using less effort.

The force that is needed to push, pull, or lift an object is called the **effort force.** The force that is holding the object in place is called the load force. To make an object move, a machine must work harder than the load force.

When a machine makes work easier, we say that it gives us a mechanical advantage [muh-KAN-uh-kuhl ad-VAN-tij]. The machine gives us a mechanical advantage because it allows us to use less force or to change the direction of the force that is needed to do work.

▲ The stairs to the tree house gives this student a mechanical advantage. She uses less effort force than the student climbing the rope to the tree house.

Identify Work

Skills Focus: observing, inferring, communicating

1. Push against the wall of your classroom. Lift your textbook off your desk. Pull your chair along the floor.

2. Draw a sketch to show each situation in step 1. Add an arrow to show the direction of your effort force in each situation. Add another arrow to show the direction that each object moved.

3. Tell a partner whether any work was done in each situation, according to the scientific definition of work.

⇨ Check Your Understanding

1. Is any work being done in this picture? Explain your answer.

2. What is a machine? How does a machine make work easier?
3. What is mechanical advantage?

Machines and the Work They Do

When you apply an effort force to a machine, the machine uses this force to do the work more quickly or more easily than you could have done it without the machine. Think of the weight that this giant crane can lift. An effort force is applied to the crane to help it lift the container.

◀ Machines can easily do work that humans would find difficult or impossible.

Machines don't have to be big or complicated to do work for us. If you've used a wheelbarrow, you know it allows you to move heavy objects more easily than you could move them with your arms alone. In fact, all machines—no matter how complicated they are—are combinations of six simple machines. The six **simple machines** that are used to make all other machines are

- the lever
- the pulley
- the wedge
- the wheel and axle
- the inclined plane
- the screw

Lever

Wheel and axle

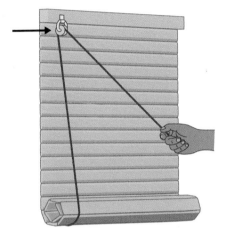

Pulley

Inclined plane

Wedge

Screw

▲ We use simple machines to move things, to lift things, to hold things together, or to push things apart. Which machines on this page are used to move things? Which machines are used to lift things, to hold things together, or to push things apart?

Simple machines can provide a mechanical advantage by changing the effect of the effort force you use. Some simple machines make work easier by allowing you to use less effort force to move an object. For example, you use less effort force to lift a car using a jack than you would if you tried to lift the car on your own. Some simple machines make work easier by changing the direction of a force. If you use a rope thrown over a tree branch to lift an object, you pull down on the rope but the object moves up. Simple machines can also move forces from one place to another. The chain on a bicycle moves the effort force from the pedals to the wheels of the bicycle.

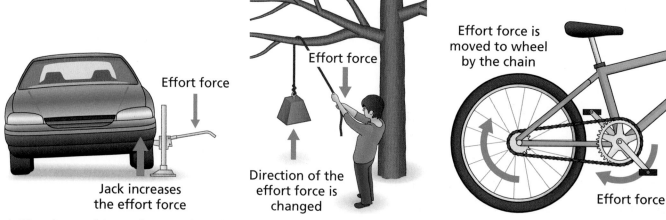

Effort force

Jack increases the effort force

Effort force

Direction of the effort force is changed

Effort force is moved to wheel by the chain

Effort force

▲ Simple machines change the effect of the effort force you use.

⇨ Check Your Understanding

1. Name the six simple machines. Give two examples of each simple machine. Try to think of at least one example of each simple machine that was not mentioned in this section.

2. What simple machines can you identify in this tool?

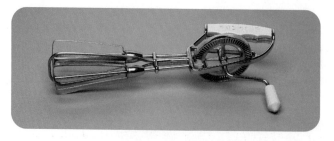

Levers

▲ Lifting a load without a lever is much harder work than lifting a load with a lever.

It would be very difficult to lift a gigantic boulder or open a can of paint with only your fingers. To make these jobs easier, we use a simple machine called a lever. A **lever** is a straight rod or board that turns around a fixed point. A lever makes work easier by making a load easier to lift.

Levers require three things to do work:
- effort force: the force you apply to the lever
- load: the object you want to move
- **fulcrum** [FUL-kruhm]: the fixed point on which the lever turns

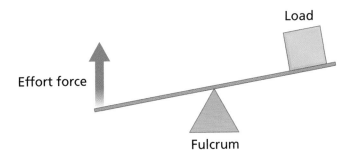

Load

Effort force

Fulcrum

◄ A lever

There are three different classes of levers. Each class of lever is used to do a different type of work and provides a different mechanical advantage.

Class of lever	Mechanical advantage	Example
first-class lever 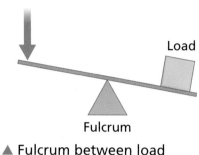 ▲ Fulcrum between load and effort	A first-class lever gives you a mechanical advantage by changing the direction of the force you use. When you use effort force to push or pull in one direction, the load travels in the other direction.	seesaw 
second-class lever 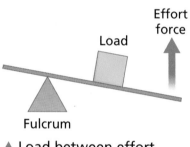 ▲ Load between effort and fulcrum	A second-class lever gives you a mechanical advantage by allowing you to use less effort force to lift an object. With a second-class lever, the direction of the effort force and the load remains the same. When you use effort force in one direction, the load travels in the same direction.	bottle opener 
third-class lever 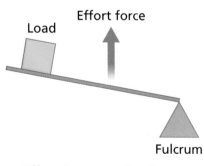 ▲ Effort between load and fulcrum	A third-class lever gives you a mechanical advantage by increasing the speed and distance you are able to move the load. The direction of the effort force and the load remains the same. When you use effort force in one direction, the load travels in the same direction.	fishing rod 

40

Build and Use Levers

Skills Focus: observing, measuring, inferring, communicating

1. Use a spring scale to measure the force required to lift an object, such as a small block.

2. Using a ruler and a marker, create a first-class, second-class, or third-class lever. Use your lever to lift your object.
   - For the first-class lever, place the fulcrum midway between the load (the object you are lifting) and the spring scale. Use the spring scale to pull down on the lever.
   - For the second-class lever, place the load midway between the fulcrum and the spring scale.
   - For the third-class lever, place the spring scale midway between the load and the fulcrum. You will have to hold the fulcrum in place.

3. Compare the effort force of lifting the object using your lever with the effort force of lifting the object not using your lever. How much effort was saved?

4. Experiment with the amount of space between the load, fulcrum, and spring scale for each lever. How can you use the least effort for each lever?

5. As a class, compare the mechanical advantage of each lever. You must be able to describe and name the type of lever you built.

   Sometimes two levers work together. A nutcracker is an example of two second-class levers. Scissors are an example of two first-class levers. Can you think of two other examples of levers working together?

⇨ Check Your Understanding

1. What class of lever is shown in each picture?

2. Describe the mechanical advantages that levers can give you.

Wheels and Axles

Rollers were the earliest form of the wheel and axle. Rollers were used by the ancient Egyptians to move the large blocks of stone they used to build the pyramids.

A wheel and axle is a simple machine that can help you move, turn, or lift an object. It has a **wheel** that turns around a rod. The rod is called an **axle.** A wheel and axle is like a lever that can rotate in a circle. The axle in the centre of the wheel is the fulcrum of the lever.

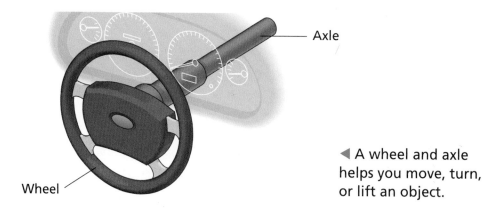

Axle

Wheel

◀ A wheel and axle helps you move, turn, or lift an object.

Moving with a Wheel and Axle

A wheel and axle can be used to move things. Cars and bicycles use wheels and axles to move. The effort force is at the axle, and the load is on a wheel. When the axle turns, the wheel also turns because they are attached. When the axle turns one time, the wheel also turns one time. Since the wheel is larger than the axle, a small turn of the axle creates a much larger turn of the wheel. This is the mechanical advantage of a wheel and axle.

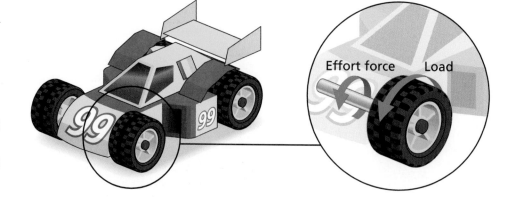

Effort force   Load

▶ Car wheels are attached to an axle. When the axle turns, the wheels turn and move the car.

Turning with a Wheel and Axle

A wheel and axle can be used to turn things. For example, a wheel and axle is what makes a doorknob work. The knob is the wheel, and the load is the axle inside the door. You use a doorknob by putting the effort force on the wheel. This turns the axle.

Do you think the size of the knob makes a difference? Is it easier to open a door using a knob that is the size of a pea or the size of an orange? The size of the knob changes the amount of effort force you have to use. When the wheel (the knob) is larger than the axle, you use less effort force to make the axle turn. So, a larger doorknob makes it easier to open the door.

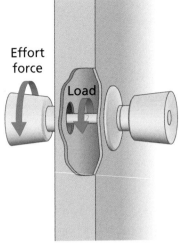

▲ You open a door by putting effort force on the doorknob to turn the axle inside the door.

Lifting with a Wheel and Axle

A wheel and axle can be used to lift things. A well has this type of wheel and axle to lift water in a pail. The handle makes a complete circle when it turns, just like a wheel. You use effort force on the wheel while the load is on the axle. The wheel and axle gives you a mechanical advantage because it allows you to lift a heavy pail of water with less force, although you have to turn the handle several times to get the pail to the top.

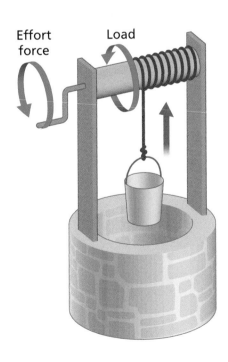

Effort force   Load

◀ You can lift a pail of water using a wheel and axle.

↪ **Learning Tip**

The diagrams in this chapter will help you understand how simple machines work. First read the explanation of how the simple machine works. Then look carefully at the diagram. Make sure that you understand what is shown. If an idea still isn't clear, reread the paragraph, then look at the diagram again until the meaning is clear.

Lift with a Wheel and Axle

Skills Focus: creating models, observing, communicating

1. Work with a partner. Punch two holes, directly across from each other, in a paper cup. Place a bendable straw through the two holes. Bend the short end of the straw up.

2. Take a 30 cm piece of string, and tie one end around a washer. Tie or tape the other end to the straw, as shown in the photo.

3. Slowly turn the short end of the straw. What happens to the washer? What happens to the straw?

4. Discuss your observations with another pair of students. What part of the set-up was the wheel? What part was the axle?

⇨ Check Your Understanding

1. Describe three ways that a wheel and axle can be used to make work easier.

2. List or sketch wheels and axles that you have used at home or at school. Group them according to the three jobs they can do.

Pulleys

A **pulley** is a rope or chain that is wrapped around a grooved wheel. When the rope or chain is pulled, the wheel turns. Pulleys make it easier to lift objects.

There are three different types of pulleys: fixed pulleys, movable pulleys, and combined pulleys.

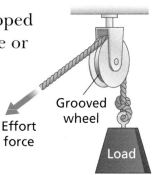

◀ A pulley is a simple machine that makes lifting easier.

Fixed Pulleys

A fixed pulley has the wheel attached to the ceiling or to another object that does not move. Since the pulley does not move, it is called a fixed pulley.

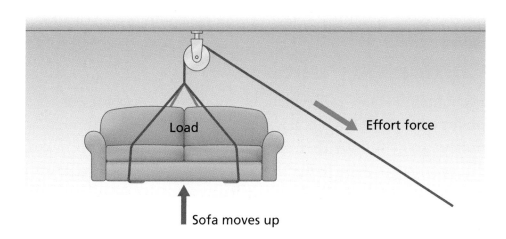

◀ A fixed pulley

A fixed pulley gives you a mechanical advantage because you change the direction of your effort force. When you pull down on the rope, the load goes up. This is very useful when you are trying to lift a heavy object. If you are trying to lift a sofa, pulling down on the rope is easier than lifting the sofa with your hands. However, with only one pulley, you still use the same amount of effort force you would have used without the pulley. You also have to pull the rope the same distance that the object is lifted. To lift the sofa 1 m, you must pull down 1 m of rope.

→Learning Tip

Look at the three diagrams of pulley systems. Ask yourself, "How are they different? How are they the same?"

Movable Pulleys

When you attach a pulley to a load you are trying to lift, you create a movable pulley. You attach one end of the rope to the ceiling and pull the other end. The pulley moves when the load is lifted. A movable pulley requires less effort force to lift the load because some of the load is supported by the ceiling.

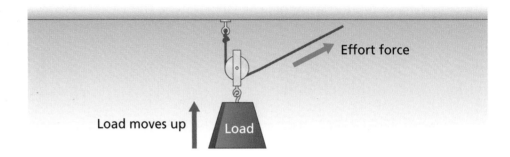

► A movable pulley

There are disadvantages to a movable pulley. When you use a movable pulley, you pull in the same direction as the load being lifted. As well, you have to use the effort force for twice the distance. To lift the load 1 m, you have to pull 2 m of rope.

Combined Pulleys

Fixed and movable pulleys can be combined. A combined pulley is also called a block and tackle. When you combine pulleys, you combine their mechanical advantage. A combined pulley allows you to change the direction and to use less effort force. The fixed pulley allows the load to move in the opposite direction of the effort force. The movable pulley reduces the effort force needed to move the load because half of the load is supported by the ceiling.

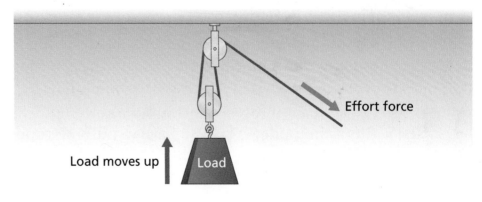

► A combined pulley

46

Try This

Measure the Effort Force

Skills Focus: measuring

1. Use a spring scale to measure the effort force needed to lift a can 10 cm.

2. Now measure the effort force required to lift the can 10 cm using a fixed pulley, a movable pulley, and a combined pulley. For each type of pulley,
   - sketch the pulley system you built
   - record the effort force needed to lift the can
   - record the amount of string needed to lift the can

3. Compare the effort force of lifting the can using each pulley with the effort force of lifting the can not using a pulley. How much effort was saved by using each pulley?

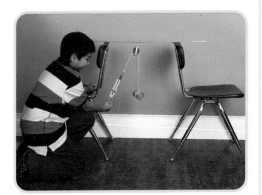

⇨ Check Your Understanding

1. What kind of pulley is being shown in each picture: fixed, movable, or combined?

 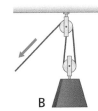 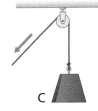

A   B   C

2. In your notebook, make a table like the one below. Complete the table to show what you have learned about pulleys.
   Hint: You will leave one box empty!

Type of pulley	Sketch of pulley	Mechanical advantage of pulley	Disadvantage of pulley

Inclined Planes and Wedges

Inclined Planes

Try This

Find the Easiest Route

Skills Focus: observing, inferring

1. Look at the picture. The two runners are of the same skill level and travel at the same speed. Which runner will get to the top of the mountain first? Which runner will travel the farthest?

2. Which route would you take? Explain why.

500 m

A   B

An **inclined plane** is a sloped surface, such as a ramp. It lets you move something to a higher level more easily than you could lift it. For example, moving a wagon filled with rocks up an inclined plane is easier than lifting the wagon the same distance. An inclined plane is different from other simple machines because it does not move. Instead, an object is moved on the inclined plane. Inclined planes that you may have seen include stairs, wheelchair ramps, and ladders.

▲ These inclined planes allow you to use less effort force to move to a higher level.

An inclined plane gives you a mechanical advantage because you use less effort force to raise an object. The less sloped the inclined plane is, the less force you need to raise the object. The disadvantage is that you must move the object a greater distance. An inclined plane allows you to raise a large load with little effort force, but you need to move the load over a greater distance.

In the Try This activity, runner B would use less effort to travel up the zigzag trail because the inclined planes are not as steep. However, the zigzag trail is a greater distance than the trail that goes straight up the mountain.

Wedges

 Try This

Use an Ulu

Skills Focus: creating models, inferring, communicating

1. The Inuit [IN-oo-eet] people of the Canadian Arctic have used ulus for more than 1000 years. An ulu [OO-loo] is a cutting tool that has many uses, such as removing the fur from animals or taking the skin off fish. Look carefully at the shape of the ulu in the picture on the right. Notice the shape of the blade and the way the handle is attached.

2. Use cardboard or Bristol board to create a model of an ulu. Hold your model in your hand, and move it to see how it might be used to remove the fur from an animal or the skin from a salmon. Show a partner how you think this tool is used.

A **wedge** is a simple machine with a thick end and a thin end. Its pointed (thin) end is used to lift, hold, or push objects apart. A wedge is similar to an inclined plane, except the wedge usually moves to do work.

A wedge works when you push on its thickest part. This gives you a mechanical advantage by changing the direction of your force. Most wedges have a handle to make them easier to use. An ulu is an example of a wedge with a handle. A chisel [CHIZ-uhl] is another example of a wedge with a handle.

▲ The chisel that this carver is using is a wedge. The carver pushes the wedge to separate the wood.

The wedge was one of the earliest simple machines used. The first wedges were rocks or sticks shaped into arrows or spears. They were used to hunt and skin animals, and to dig in the ground. Early peoples realized that when a rock or stick was sharper, it worked better. They realized that sharpening a wedge increased its mechanical advantage because less effort force was needed to use it.

When you push down on a wedge to cut, the edge of the wedge splits the object apart. A thin wedge needs less effort force to cut than a thick wedge does.

Types of Wedges

Most wedges are two inclined planes put together. These wedges are used to split apart objects. The blade of an axe is one example of this type of wedge. Your front teeth are another example. They split food into pieces as you bite down.

Other wedges have only one inclined plane. These wedges are used to lift objects or to stop objects from moving. A doorstop is an example of this type of wedge. It is used to keep a door from moving.

▲ Your front teeth act as wedges when you bite into food.

▲ This wedge is used to stop a door from moving.

⇨ Check Your Understanding

1. What is an inclined plane?

2. Is an inclined plane the same as other simple machines? Explain.

3. How does an inclined plane make work easier? What is the disadvantage of an inclined plane?

4. Think of a wedge you use. Explain how it makes work easier.

5. Draw a picture to show how you would improve this wedge.

Screws

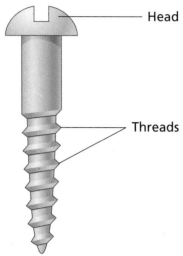

▲ A screw is an inclined plane that wraps around a centre core.

Head

Threads

Look around your classroom. What holds things, like your desk or chair, together? Many objects are held together with a simple machine called a screw. A **screw** is an inclined plane that is wrapped around a central core to form a spiral.

As you turn the head of a screw, the screw moves down into a block of wood. The screw acts like a wedge, pushing the wood apart. When the threads of a screw are closer together, you use less effort force to put the screw in the wood because the length of the inclined plane is longer. However, the increased length means that you must turn the screw more times to drive it into the wood. This is the same disadvantage that the inclined plane has—to use less effort force, you need to move a greater distance.

Over 2000 years ago, a mathematician named Archimedes invented a screw that could be used to lift water. The lower end of the screw was placed in the water. As the screw was turned, water was lifted up by the threads until it reached the top, where it poured out.

▲ An Archimedes screw

There are many examples of how a screw is used. A few examples are shown below.

▲ A spiral staircase is a screw that you can walk on to raise yourself to a higher level.

▲ If you take the cover off a pencil sharpener, you will find two screws that work together to grind away your dull pencil.

▲ Screws called propellers make travelling through air easier.

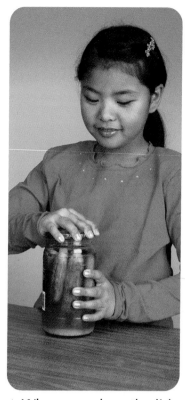

▲ When you close the lid on a pickle jar, you are using a screw to attach the lid to the jar.

⇨ Check Your Understanding

1. Which of these objects is a screw? Explain your answer.

2. What is the advantage of a screw? What is the disadvantage?

Key Idea: Work is done when a force makes an object move.

Vocabulary

work p. 33

effort force p. 34

Key Idea: A machine is anything that makes work easier for us.

Vocabulary

simple machines
  p. 36

Key Idea: Machines give us a mechanical advantage by changing the amount or direction of force needed to do work.

Key Idea: There are six simple machines: the lever, the wheel and axle, the pulley, the inclined plane, the wedge, and the screw.

Vocabulary

lever p. 39

fulcrum p. 39

wheel p. 42

axle p. 42

pulley p. 45

inclined plane
  p. 48

wedge p. 50

screw p. 52

Review Key Ideas and Vocabulary

Use the vocabulary words in your answers to the questions.

1. What does "work" mean in science? Explain whether work is being done in each of the following situations.

2. What is a machine? Explain whether each of the following objects is a machine.

  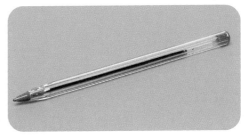

3. Describe three different examples of ways that a simple machine changes the effect of an effort force.

4. Name each simple machine.
   Give another example of each type of simple machine.

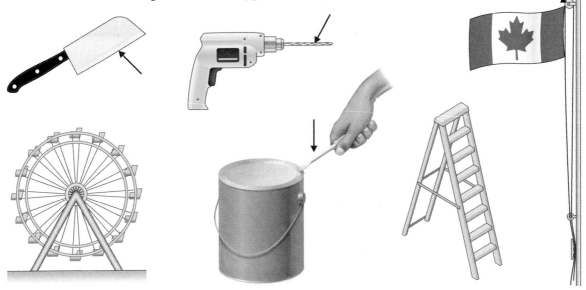

Choose the Best Machine for the Job

Looking Back

You have learned

- that machines give you a mechanical advantage by changing the amount or direction of force needed to do work
- that there are six simple machines

In this activity, you will work in a group to find out which simple machine, the lever, pulley, or inclined plane, is best to help you lift a bag of marbles.

Demonstrate Your Learning

Build and Test a Simple Machine

1. Work in a group. Your teacher will assign your group a lever, a pulley, or an inclined plane to build and test.

2. Create a table to record your observations.

3. Determine the effort force that is needed to lift a bag of marbles to a height of 30 cm without a simple machine. Record this in your notebook.

4. Build your simple machine.

5. Measure the effort force that is needed to lift the bag of marbles to a height of 30 cm with your simple machine. Record this in your notebook.

6. Experiment with variations of your simple machine. For example, change the placement of the fulcrum when you build a first-class lever.

7. Repeat step 5. Did the effort force change? If it did, record the new measurement in your table. If it didn't, write "no change."

Evaluate

1. Compare your results with other groups' results. Compare
   • the advantages and disadvantages of using a lever, pulley, and inclined plane
   • the effort force required to lift the bag of marbles
   • the effort force saved

2. Which simple machine saved the greatest effort force—the lever, the pulley, or the inclined plane?

Communicate

1. Create a brochure promoting the best machine for lifting heavy objects. In your brochure, be sure to
   • describe the advantages of using this machine to lift an object
   • include how much effort force it saves
   • include how that machine can be used to do work

⇨ **Assessment Checklist**

SIMPLE MACHINE
As you build and test your simple machine, make sure that you show you are able to

✔ use a spring scale correctly
✔ experiment with variations of your simple machine
✔ accurately record your observations
✔ use appropriate scientific words
✔ communicate clearly

We use simple and compound machines to do work for us.

▶ Simple machines can be combined to form compound machines.

▶ Compound machines combine the mechanical advantage of two or more simple machines.

▶ Simple and compound machines are used in our daily lives.

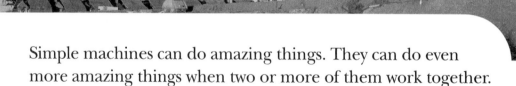

Simple machines can do amazing things. They can do even more amazing things when two or more of them work together.

Look at the giant mining machine in this picture. This machine is one of the largest machines in the world and it does many kinds of work. The bucket wheel digs the soil. The soil is moved along the machine on a rolling inclined plane and then put into waiting trucks. What other simple machine can you see in it?

In this chapter, you will learn how simple machines can be combined. You will learn about the important jobs that machines do in communities throughout British Columbia. Then you will use your problem-solving skills to design and build your own machine.

Compound Machines

Simple machines can be combined to make work easier. A machine that is made up of two or more simple machines is called a **compound machine.** A compound machine combines the mechanical advantages of at least two simple machines.

A shovel is an example of a compound machine. It is a wedge and a lever combined. The edge of the shovel is the wedge. It changes the amount of effort force needed to dig in the snow. The sharper the wedge is, the more easily it can dig. The shovel handle is a third-class lever. When you use a shovel, the hand that holds the handle is the fulcrum and the other hand provides the effort force. With a short movement of your fulcrum hand, you can lift the load (the snow) a long way in the direction of the effort force. Most of the machines you use to do work are really combinations of more than one simple machine.

> **⇨ Learning Tip**
>
> Check your understanding of compound machines. In your own words, explain to a partner how a shovel is an example of a compound machine.

Fulcrum

Effort force

Load

Wedge

▲ A shovel combines the mechanical advantage of a wedge and the mechanical advantage of a lever.

When you use a compound machine, you can change either the size or the direction of the effort force you apply to the machine. Some compound machines change both the size and the direction of the effort force.

Common Compound Machines

Look at two compound machines you know well—scissors and a can opener. The arms on the scissors are two levers that cross each other. The blades are two wedges that work together to cut. A screw is sometimes used to hold the scissors together.

Learning Tip

Use the pictures to check your understanding of the paragraph above them. Look at each picture, then read each caption until you are sure you understand what is described in the caption.

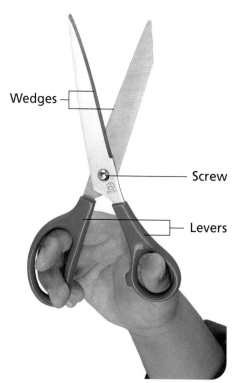

Wedges

Screw

Levers

▲ Scissors combine the mechanical advantages of three simple machines: a lever, a wedge, and a screw.

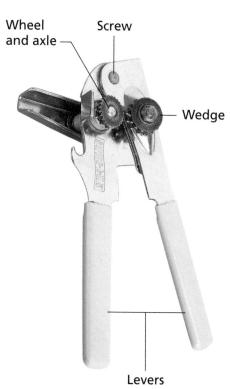

Wheel and axle

Screw

Wedge

Levers

▲ A can opener is a compound machine. Notice the two levers, the wedge, the wheel and axle system, and the screw.

The can opener is made of two levers, a wedge, a wheel and axle system, and a screw. When you apply force to squeeze the two levers, the wedge cuts into the can. The wheel and axle system moves the wedge along the rim of the can. The screw holds the pieces of the can opener together.

Cars and bicycles are also compound machines, but the simple machines in them may be hard to identify. If you look really carefully at a car or bicycle, you should be able to see screws, levers, wheels and axles, and other simple machines.

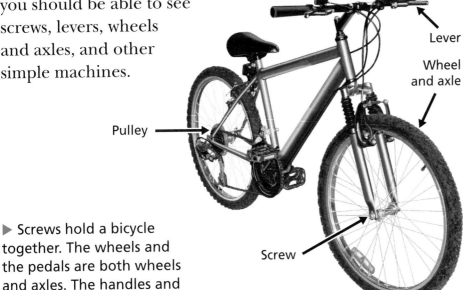

Lever

Wheel and axle

Pulley

Screw

▶ Screws hold a bicycle together. The wheels and the pedals are both wheels and axles. The handles and the gear shift are levers.

 Try This

Examine Compound Machines

Skills Focus: observing

1. Your teacher will provide several compound machines for you to examine.

2. Work with a partner to identify the simple machines that make up these compound machines.

⇨ Check Your Understanding

1. Identify the simple machines in this compound machine.

2. Why do we use compound machines? Name two compound machines you use that aren't mentioned in this section.

The Power of Compound Machines

As you have learned, there are several simple machines, such as a pulley, an inclined plane, a lever, and a wheel and axle, that can be used to lift a heavy load. Each of these simple machines makes lifting easier by allowing you to use less effort force, by increasing the distance over which the effort force is used, or by changing the direction of your effort force.

> **⇨ Learning Tip**
>
> Look carefully at the three pictures in this section and read the captions. What are the advantages and disadvantages of each method shown?

▲ When you use an inclined plane, you need less effort force to lift an object but you have to use this force over a greater distance.

▲ When you use a fixed pulley, you can change the direction of your effort force by pulling down to lift an object.

When an inclined plane and a fixed pulley are combined into a compound machine, their mechanical advantages are combined. You use less effort force pulling in one direction, while the load moves along the inclined plane in another direction. When wheels are added to the bottom of the object being moved, the effort force is reduced even more.

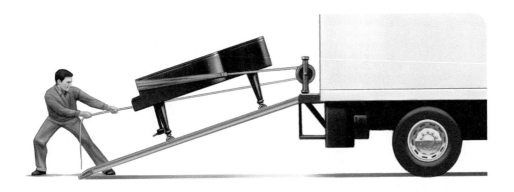

◄ When you use a compound machine, you combine the mechanical advantages of two or more simple machines.

Try This

Combine Mechanical Advantages

Skills Focus: classifying

1. Think of a simple machine, such as an inclined plane, that allows you to use less effort force by increasing the distance the force moves through.

2. Think of another simple machine, such as a screw, that allows you to use less effort force by changing the direction of the force.

3. Think of a way to link the two simple machines to form a compound machine. Draw a picture of your compound machine. Write a sentence explaining how the mechanical advantages are combined.

⇨ Check Your Understanding

1. Identify the mechanical advantages you would have if you used a compound machine that combined
   - a fixed pulley with a wheel and axle
   - a first class lever with a wedge

Awesome SCIENCE

Amazing Robots

▲ This robot can walk down stairs and respond to some human commands.

Robots are very complex compound machines. They are controlled by computer programs that tell them how to move. Because robots can be controlled, they can do work for us. Robots come in many forms, depending on the job they do.

▲ Robots don't become tired or bored, so they can do the same job all day.

Robots do different jobs. Many robots work in factories. They have a "hand" that is a built-in tool, such as a drill, screwdriver, or grasping fingers. The hand is used to do a specific job. Some robots are sent into space. For example, the Canadarm on the space shuttle and the Mars Rover are sent into space to help humans learn about the solar system. Robots are also sent to places that are too dangerous for humans, such as inside a volcano. These robots carry cameras and other instruments to collect information. Robots are even used in medicine. For example, robotic arms, with their careful and accurate movements, are used with cameras to help doctors perform very delicate operations.

Robotic Arms

Many robots copy the movements of a human arm. Your arm works as a third-class lever. The bone in your lower arm is the lever. The joint at your elbow is the fulcrum. The bicep muscle, which is attached to your bone, controls the effort. Your hand, and anything you might have in it, is the load. When you want to lift your fork to eat, your brain sends a message to contract the bicep muscle on the bone. When the bicep muscle contracts, it creates a force that pulls up the bone to raise your fork. A robotic arm works in a similar way. Instead of a brain, however, the robot's computer controls the arm. A robotic arm can be made to lift, move, and hold objects.

Many people now have artificial arms that can be controlled by their nervous system. An artificial arm has a sensor that sends signals to the brain. The brain then sends signals to the muscles. Sensors on the muscles tell the arm how to move. Understanding how the human arm works has allowed scientists and doctors to create artificial arms that give people freedom and independence.

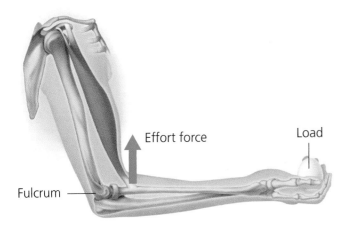

Effort force

Load

Fulcrum

▲ Both a human arm and a robotic arm work as third-class levers.

▲ With an artificial arm, this mountain biker is able to control the movement of his bike when riding down the trail.

Compound Machines over Time

Since early times, people have found new ways to combine simple machines in order to make work easier and faster. Over time, compound machines have become much more complex and powerful. Here are some of these changes to compound machines.

▲ Early horse-drawn ploughs used a simple wedge and a lever to dig the ground.

▲ Today, a tractor-pulled plough allows a farmer in the Fraser Valley to do as much work in one day as a team of farmers and horse-drawn ploughs would have taken many days to complete.

▲ An early method of travelling through the water was the canoe. A cedar canoe moves quickly through the water. The paddle acts as a lever and the narrow bow as a wedge.

▲ Today's power boats use a powerful propeller, which is a screw connected to a wheel and axle. They combine this with a gas-powered engine to speed through the water.

▲ In the early 1900s people had to work hard to clear land and build roads with simple hand tools such as picks, shovels, and rakes.

▲ Today, large machines called graders are used to help build roads. The large wheels of the grader move easily over rough ground as the blade, acting as a wedge, pushes layers of soil. The operator in the cab of the grader moves a lever to lift the blade or change its angle.

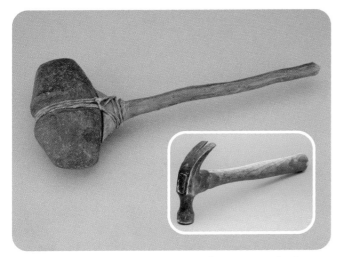

▲ The earliest hammers were levers made from rocks tied to wooden or bone handles. Later, metal hammers were made by blacksmiths. These hammers had a flat face for driving nails and two wedges, called a claw, for pulling nails out of wood.

▲ Today, nail guns are replacing hammers. When a worker pushes the trigger lever of a modern nail gun, air within the nail gun drives the nail into the wood. This is faster and needs a lot less effort force than using a hammer does.

⇨ Check Your Understanding

1. In what ways have the machines that people use changed over time?

Compound Machines in Mining

For more than 150 years, coal has been mined in the Crowsnest Pass area of southeastern British Columbia. The machines that are used to remove the coal from the mountains have changed a lot over time.

Early Mining

Early mining machinery needed the physical strength of people and animals to do work. Early miners in British Columbia went deep into tunnels, carrying compound machines such as shovels and pickaxes. The miners worked in small, damp tunnels to dig the coal. Once the coal had been dug, they moved it by hand to larger tunnels and then shovelled it into wheeled carts. The wheeled carts were pushed by hand or pulled out of the mine by horses. While the wheeled carts provided a mechanical advantage over moving the coal by hand, the work was slow and required a lot of physical strength.

▲ Machines used in the early days of mining in British Columbia depended on the physical strength of the miners that worked with them.

Mining Today

Mining coal in British Columbia is very different today. Many mines are large open pits, rather than tunnels. Powerful machines have replaced much of the physical effort that was needed in the past. For example, the operator of a giant backhoe uses a system of levers in the cab to make the power shovel move. The arm on the backhoe is a third-class lever. The attached shovel is used as a wedge to dig and then is lifted up by a pulley to load the coal into the truck.

▲ Mining at the Gibralter Mine, near Williams Lake, is done with powerful machines. Coal is moved with less effort and greater speed because of the mechanical advantages of compound machines such as backhoes and dump trucks.

Conveyor Belts

Huge conveyor [kuhn-VEY-er] belts at processing plants are used to move the coal. A conveyor belt moves the coal through cleaning machines to remove the unwanted rock from the coal. Once cleaned, the coal is moved by conveyor belts to a dryer and then moved up into huge silos [SIE-lowz] to be stored. The coal is transported by train to the coast, where conveyor belts are used once again to load large ships.

A conveyor belt is a compound machine. It works by combining the mechanical advantage of wheels and axles with the mechanical advantage of a moving inclined plane.

▲ At the Port of Vancouver, gigantic conveyor belts load the coal into a waiting ship.

 Try This

Build a Conveyor Belt

Skills Focus: creating models

1. Make a conveyor belt using simple materials. Think about how a wheel and axle and an inclined plane can be combined. Can you think of another simple machine that you could add to make your conveyor belt operate?

 Be very careful when using the hammer and nails. Wear safety goggles while building your machine.

⇨ Check Your Understanding

⇨ Learning Tip

Locate the information you need to fill in this table by rereading the section and looking at the photos.

1. Copy the following table into your notebook. Complete the table to describe how compound machines were used and are now used in mining.

Use of compound machines	Then	Now
to lift coal		
to move coal		
to load coal		

2. Some mining in British Columbia is still done in tunnels. Today, however, a powerful drill is used instead of a pickaxe. What simple machines can you identify in this compound machine?

Compound Machines in Forestry

Compound machines, such as the feller buncher, can cut down trees faster and with less physical effort than the saws and axes used by early loggers. Most feller bunchers have a third-class lever arm, similar to the backhoe used in mining. A logger in the cab uses hand levers to move the machine's arm into place, to turn on the saw that cuts down the tree, and then to place the log into a waiting logging truck.

▲ Driven on large tracks, a feller buncher surrounds a tree with its massive jaws and then makes a cut through the trunk using a saw.

▲ Early loggers in Vancouver created a platform by inserting springboards into cuts in a tree. Then they used their sharpened wedges, axes, and saws to cut down the tree.

Some forestry machines run on tracks, and others have wheels. Tracks allow machines to move more easily over rough ground. The machines have better grip in wet areas than machines with wheels, and they move easily up and down hills. The tracks reduce damage to the ground because they carry the weight of a machine over a larger surface area. Machines with wheels are able to move faster than machines that run on tracks. As well, they are easier to move and able to make tighter turns.

Once the logs are loaded into a truck, they are sent to sawmills. There, giant cranes use a pulley system to move the logs onto conveyor belts. The moving inclined planes move the logs through machines that saw them into usable wood called lumber. The lumber is then moved by train or truck to be sold.

▲ Large trucks are used to lift and move logs around the sawmill.

▲ Large trucks are used to transport the finished lumber products.

⇨ Check Your Understanding

1. Describe how machines used to harvest trees have changed over time.
2. List two advantages of using machines with wheels. List two advantages of using machines that run on tracks.

ScienceWorks

Carving Using Simple and Compound Machines

Have you ever heard of the Loch Ness monster? Did you know that British Columbia has its own creature, believed to live deep down in Okanagan Lake?

The people of the Okanagan First Nation have many stories and legends about this creature, called N'ha'a'itk [nuh-haw-aw-it-ck]. N'ha'a'itk means "snake of the lake" in the Okanagan language. Students at a school in the Central Okanagan School District learned about the legend of N'ha'a'itk, or Ogopogo as it is more commonly known, at the same time that they learned about the techniques, tools, and traditions of carving.

John Yeltatzie is a master Haida [HY-duh] carver from Haida Gwaii (Queen Charlotte Islands). He lives in the Okanagan and works part time for the Central Okanagan School District as an Artist in Residence. Mr. Yeltatzie spends his time teaching students at the school about the importance of carving in the lives of First Nations peoples. Carving is a way that First Nations peoples, especially those on the west coast of British Columbia, record their history.

▲ Mr. Yeltatzie explains about Haida carving to a group of students.

The students at the school worked with Mr. Yeltatzie to create a carving of N'ha'a'itk. Together, they chipped away the wood from a yellow cedar pole. Mr. Yeltatzie had an Okanagan Elder come in to explain the legend of N'ha'a'itk as the carving was being done.

▲ The carving of N'ha'a'itk

The carving of N'ha'a'itk is now on permanent display in the school. The carving has a "very beautiful face" and "looks amazing," says Audrey Barr, an Aboriginal Advocate at the school where the carving took place. Aboriginal Advocates provide support to Aboriginal students and their families in the school system.

N'ha'a'itk was carved in the traditional Haida style. The Haida style is quite detailed and difficult. The students at the school worked very hard to learn the different skills they needed.

Traditionally, Aboriginal carvers used simple machines:

- Stone axes were used to split the logs.

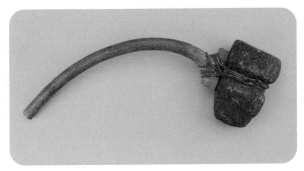

▲ An early stone axe

- Stone adzes [ADZ-z] were used to make the rough shape of the carving.

▲ An early stone adze

- Drills were used to make holes in the wood. These holes could be used to tie or hold different pieces together. These types of early drills were considered simple machines.

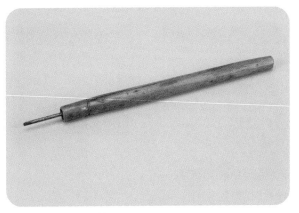

▲ An early drill

- Knives were used to carve out the details. The knives were made of stone, bone, or shell, and came in many different shapes and sizes. They were made to fit the carver's hand.

▲ An early knife

Today, Aboriginal carvers use metal tools and modern compound machines to create their artwork. The power saw can be used to cut wood into pieces. However, the traditions around carving are as important now as they were hundreds of years ago.

 Nisga'a Fish Wheel

▲ The Nass River is in northern British Columbia.

A fish wheel is an example of a machine that has been used by Aboriginal peoples of British Columbia for many generations. This traditional fishing method is still used today because it is able to do the work quickly and easily.

◄ A fish wheel uses the force of moving water to turn an axle. Baskets attached to the axle fill with fish as the wheel turns.

A fish wheel is a compound machine that uses the force of moving water. The wheel sits on a floating structure in a river where the moving water provides steady power to the wheel. Four large baskets are attached to the axle, with one of the baskets under the water. The pushing force of the moving water makes the basket under the water move. This turns the axle, which turns the wheel, causing another basket to enter the water. The wheel continues to turn around and around because of the pushing force of the water. Fish are caught in the baskets as they swim with the current. They are lifted from the water in the rising baskets, and then fall down an inclined plane into a live pen located outside the floating fish wheel.

The Nisga'a [nis-gaa] fish wheel is a fishing machine that works better than many modern fishing machines. It is a gentle machine that prevents damage to fish that is normally caused by hooks and nets on large fishing boats. The fish are fresh because they are kept alive in the pens until ready for processing. The fishers can select the fish they want to keep, and then release young fish or types of fish they don't want to keep.

The Nisga'a people also use the fish wheel to help them understand salmon migration and fish populations in the Nass River. Some of the fish are captured, measured, tagged, and then released back into the river to continue their migration. If tagged fish are recaptured later, the information on the tags is used to help scientists understand how many salmon survive and where the salmon migrate. In this way, the fish wheel is much more than just a method of collecting fish. It is an important tool that provides scientific information about the number of salmon in the Nass River.

◀ Nisga'a fishers catching salmon on the Nass River.

⏵ **Learning Tip**

Use questions to check your understanding of each paragraph in this section. Ask yourself, "How does a Nisga'a fish wheel work? In what ways is it better than other fishing methods? What else is it used for?"

⏵ Check Your Understanding

1. Sketch the Nisga'a fish wheel. Label all the simple machines you can see.

2. How do you think the fish wheel has changed in the last 100 years?

3. What advantages does the fish wheel have over modern fishing machines?

Chapter Review

We use simple and compound machines to do work for us.

Key Idea: Simple machines can be combined to form compound machines.

Vocabulary

compound machine p. 59

Key Idea: Compound machines combine the mechanical advantage of two or more simple machines.

Key Idea: Simple and compound machines are used in our daily lives.

Review Key Ideas and Vocabulary

Use the vocabulary words in your answers to the questions.

1. What is a compound machine? Is a pair of pliers a simple machine or a compound machine? Explain your answer.

2. Use the picture below to explain why people use compound machines instead of just simple machines.

3. Name two compound machines that you often use. Name at least two simple machines in each machine you listed.

4. Name the simple machines in each compound machine shown.

Apply What You've Learned

How We Use Machines: Then and Now

Looking Back

You have learned
- that simple machines can be combined to form compound machines
- how compound machines are used in our daily lives to make jobs easier

In this activity, you will research how our use of machines has changed over time.

Demonstrate Your Learning

Research the Use of Machines

1. Choose an activity in British Columbia's history that required the use of simple or compound machines.

You can choose an activity of Aboriginal peoples or early settlers in British Columbia. Think of machines that were used to harvest resources, to transport people or things, or to make work easier in some way. For example, you might choose one of the following activities:

- carving canoes
- cutting down trees
- raising totem poles
- fishing
- mining
- transportation
- preserving or preparing food
- building homes

2. Use books or the Internet, or both, to find information about the use of machines in the activity you chose. Ask Aboriginal Elders or talk to local senior citizens about what they remember from earlier times.

Communicate

1. Make a poster showing how the use of machines in the activity you chose has changed over time. Use the headings "Then" and "Now" on your poster. Under each heading, draw or paste pictures that show the machines being used. Write one paragraph below each picture to describe how the simple or compound machine was used in the past or is used now.

⇨ Assessment Checklist

RESEARCH AND COMMUNICATE

As you research the use of machines in past and present British Columbia, make sure that you show you are able to

✔ use information from at least three resources
✔ clearly identify the simple and compound machines used
✔ describe how the machines were used in the activity you chose
✔ use photographs or drawings to illustrate the machines used
✔ communicate clearly with others

Design a Compound Machine

Looking Back

In this unit, you have learned
- how forces affect the way that objects move
- that there are six simple machines
- that simple machines can be combined to form compound machines

In this activity, you will use your understanding of the mechanical advantages of simple machines to design a compound machine that will make an everyday household task easier.

Demonstrate Your Learning

Plan

1. Choose a task for your compound machine to accomplish. For example, your compound machine could
   - make a bed
   - open a window
   - lift something out of a drawer or off the floor
   - move an egg from the refrigerator to a frying pan

2. Think about what you have learned. Identify two or more simple machines that could be combined to do the task you chose.

Design

1. Draw a full-page sketch of your compound machine. Label each simple machine you would use. Next to each label, describe how the simple machine will make the task easier.

2. If possible, build your compound machine or a model of your compound machine. Then test how it works.

 If you are using woodworking equipment, such as hammers, nails, and screwdrivers, wear safety goggles and ask an adult to supervise.

3. Explain your machine to at least one other classmate. Ask for feedback and make necessary changes and improvements to your machine based on the feedback.

Communicate

1. Create a marketing brochure for your machine. Include
   • the task that your machine can perform
   • a detailed illustration of your machine in action

⇨ Assessment Checklist

COMPOUND MACHINE
Your design should show that you are able to

✔ identify a task that a compound machine can make easier
✔ accurately identify simple machines
✔ describe how each simple machine makes the task easier to perform
✔ show how compound machines are made up of simple machines

MARKETING BROCHURE
Your brochure should show that you are able to

✔ communicate clearly with others

Preview

The human body is an amazing "machine." It may look simple from the outside—two arms, two legs, and a head, all attached to a body. However, the human body is actually made of millions of tiny parts that work together to make everything you do possible, from scratching your nose to doing a karate side thrust kick. How does it do all these things?

In this unit, you will discover how the parts of your body are organized into systems and learn about the important jobs that each system does. You will discover how your body takes in food, water, and oxygen and sends them to every part of your body. You will learn how your body's bones and muscles make it possible for you to move. You will also learn how your brain acts as a control centre, making sure that all the systems in your body work together to keep you alive and healthy.

Classify Body Parts

Skills Focus: classifying

1. With a partner, make a list of all the parts of your body that you know about. Think about the parts you can see, as well as the parts you cannot see.

2. On a large sheet of paper, classify your body parts into groups. For example, you might group your body parts according to the jobs they do in your body or their locations in your body. Give each group a title.

3. Compare your groups of body parts with other students' groups of body parts. How are they the same? How are they different?

◀ Your body is made up of many systems that work together to keep you healthy and active.

Chapter 4

Your body takes in nutrients and oxygen to keep you alive.

Key Ideas

▶ Your body is made of different systems, and each of these systems has a job to do.

▶ Your digestive system breaks down food into nutrients.

▶ Your respiratory system takes in oxygen that your body uses to get energy from nutrients.

Like all living things, you need energy to stay alive. You need energy to move, grow, and do all the things you do every day—from sleeping and reading to running and catching. Where does this energy come from? Where does your body get the energy it needs to keep working 24 hours a day?

In this chapter, you will learn how your body takes in the water, food, and oxygen it needs through its digestive [die-JES-tihv] and respiratory [RES-puhr-uh-TOR-ee] systems. You will learn why you need these things to grow and be active.

What Is a Body System?

Did you know that your body is made of many systems? Each body system is made of parts that work together to do a job. The diagram below explains the jobs of the parts of your body. It also shows how these body parts are organized into systems.

1. Cells

Cells are the smallest parts of your body. Your body is made of billions and billions of cells. Many cells have special jobs. A muscle cell is one type of cell that has a special job.

Muscle cell

2. Tissues

Most cells form groups. These groups are called tissues. All the cells in a tissue are similar in shape and do a similar job in your body. Muscle cells form muscle tissue.

Muscle tissue

3. Organs

Different groups of tissues form the **organs** in your body. An organ carries out one or more jobs in your body. Your stomach is an organ. Muscle tissue is one of the tissues in your stomach.

Stomach

4. Systems

Your organs work together in body systems. Each body system has one main job to do to help you stay alive and healthy. Your stomach is one of the organs in your digestive system.

Digestive system

> **Learning Tip**
>
> Think about how the information in each box relates to the information in the next box. To check your understanding, describe the relationship between each pair of boxes to a partner.

Cells, tissues, and organs in each body system work together so that your body works properly.

⇨ Check Your Understanding

1. How are cells, tissues, organs, and systems related to each other?

2 Your Digestive System and How It Works

▶ Your body takes in food and digests it to keep you alive.

Your digestive system has the important job of processing food so that your body can use it. This processing of food is called **digestion** [die-JES-chuhn].

During digestion, the food you eat is broken down into smaller and smaller pieces. At the end of digestion, the cells in your body get the nutrients [NOO-tree-uhnts] they need. **Nutrients** are materials that your body needs to stay alive and grow. The cells in your body also need water. They get water from the liquids you drink and from some of the food you eat. Most fruits and vegetables have a lot of water in them.

Your digestive system has organs that work together to keep digestion going from the time food enters your mouth until the time nutrients from the food enter your cells.

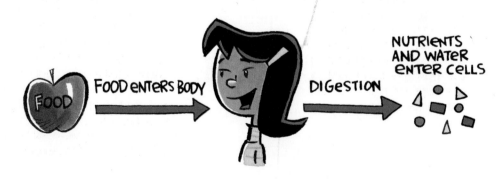

FOOD   FOOD ENTERS BODY   DIGESTION   NUTRIENTS AND WATER ENTER CELLS

▶ Digestion changes the food you eat into nutrients that your body cells can use.

Digesting an Apple

How does each organ in your digestive system help your body get the nutrients it needs from food? Let's follow an apple on its path through the digestive system to find out.

Learning Tip

Read the labels to find the organs of the digestive system. Then read about the jobs of the organs in order starting with 1.

1. The mouth is the beginning of the digestive system. Its job is to break down food so it can be swallowed. Your teeth bite and chew food until it is mushy. Your tongue moves the food around and mixes it with saliva [suh-LIE-vuh] to make it easier to swallow.

2. As you swallow, the mixture of food and saliva moves down the esophagus [ih-SAWF-uh-guhs]. The **esophagus** is a long tube that runs from your mouth to your stomach. The esophagus uses muscles to squeeze the food so that it moves down to the stomach.

Mouth

Esophagus

Stomach

Liver

3. The **stomach** is a pear-shaped organ at the end of the esophagus. It gets bigger when it is filled with food. Strong chemical juices in the stomach break down the food even more. The stomach also mixes the food. By the time the food mixture leaves your stomach, it is a thin, watery liquid.

Large intestine

Colon

5. When the nutrients have passed into the cells, there are wastes left over. These go to your large intestine. The **large intestine** is another tube, but it is much wider and shorter than the small intestine. The first part of the large intestine is called the colon [KOH-luhn]. The **colon** squeezes most of the water out of the wastes. This water is put back into your body. The solid wastes that are left exit your body through the lower part of the large intestine, called the rectum.

Pancreas

Small intestine

4. The liquid food mixture moves from your stomach into the small intestine [in-TES-tin]. The **small intestine** is a long, thin tube that winds back and forth. Chemical juices flow into the small intestine to help break down food even more. Some of these chemical juices come from the pancreas [PAN-kree-uhs], and some come from the liver. The **liver** is an organ that helps break down the fats in food. By the time the liquid reaches the end of the small intestine, it has been broken down into nutrients. These nutrients, along with water, are passed into cells in the wall of the small intestine.

Your digestive system uses a chemical called hydrochloric [HI-druh-KLOR-ik] acid to help break down food. Hydrochloric acid is so strong that it can dissolve paint. Besides helping your body break down food, it kills some bacteria that could make you sick.

Try This

Make a Model of the Digestive System

Skills Focus: creating models, measuring, inferring

1. Work with a group. Write the names of the following parts of the digestive system on index cards: mouth, esophagus, stomach, small intestine, large intestine.

2. Measure 9 m of string. Tape the string on your classroom floor or along a wall.

3. Beginning with the mouth, measure and mark the length of each organ listed below on the string, one after the other. Tape each index card above the correct section on the string.
   - mouth: 8 cm
   - small intestine: 7.0 m
   - esophagus: 26 cm
   - large intestine: 1.5 m
   - stomach: 16 cm

4. You have just made a model that shows the average length of the digestive system in an adult. Do you think your digestive system is the same length? Why or why not?

Check Your Understanding

1. Complete the following table by describing the jobs of each part of your digestive system when you eat an apple.

Part of digestive system	Job
mouth	
esophagus	
stomach	
small intestine	
pancreas	
liver	
large intestine	

2. Food stays in your stomach for 2 to 3 hours and in your small intestine for about 3 hours. Why do you think food stays in each organ so long?

Awesome SCIENCE

Not All Digestive Systems Are the Same!

Birds

Did you know that birds do not have any teeth? They can't chew to start breaking down food. Instead, they swallow small stones to help them digest their food. The stones go into the gizzard, where they help to break down food.

gizzard

Snakes

Most snakes have a very long esophagus. In some snakes, the esophagus can be almost half the length of the body when stretched out! The esophagus has many folds on the inside. These folds allow the esophagus to expand, which helps a snake swallow its prey whole. The muscles in the esophagus push the food down, toward the stomach.

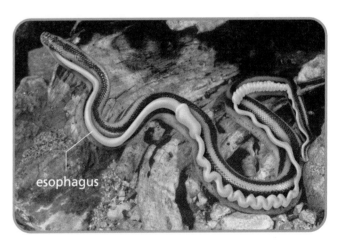

esophagus

Cows

Grass is very hard to digest, so cows have four stomachs! Each stomach plays a role in helping cows digest their food. Cows spit up food from their first stomach and chew it again to help them digest it. This is called ruminating [ROO-muh-NAYT-ing]. Most cows spend about 6 to 8 hours a day ruminating to digest and then use their food! Sheep, goats, and deer also have four stomachs.

stomachs

Your Respiratory System and How It Works

▲ The air you breathe provides you with the oxygen you need.

⇨ Learning Tip

As you read, connect what you learn to your own life. Ask yourself, "How does oxygen help keep me healthy?"

Your body needs nutrients and water to stay alive and healthy. You also need one more thing—oxygen. Without oxygen, you could only survive for a few minutes. **Oxygen** is a gas that is found in the air you breathe. Just as a fire cannot burn without oxygen, your cells cannot "burn" the fuel from the food you eat without oxygen. Your body needs oxygen to release the energy from the nutrients in your cells. Without oxygen, these nutrients would not release energy, and all the systems in your body would shut down.

How does your body get oxygen? This is the job of the respiratory system. The main organs of the respiratory system are the mouth, nose, trachea [TRAY-kee-uh], and lungs. Let's see how these organs work to bring oxygen to your cells.

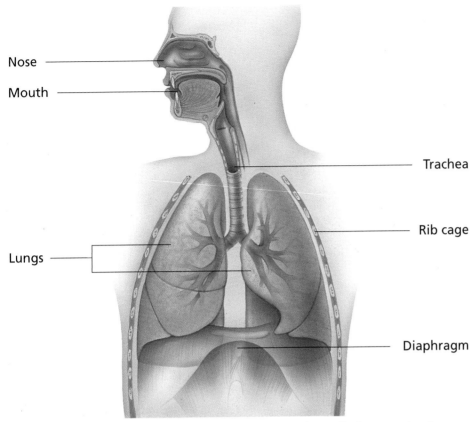

Nose

Mouth

Trachea

Rib cage

Lungs

Diaphragm

▲ Your respiratory system brings oxygen to the cells in your body.

You breathe in air through your nose or your mouth. Breathing in is called inhaling. The air travels down your throat to a tube called the **trachea.** The trachea is also called the windpipe. There is a flap over the trachea. This flap opens when you are breathing in so air can go down to your lungs. It closes if you are drinking or eating so that food or liquid does not go down the trachea.

The bottom of the trachea divides into two branches. Each branch goes into a lung. A **lung** is a spongy organ in your chest that sits inside your ribs. You have two lungs. The branch in each lung divides into smaller and smaller branches. At the end of these branches are tiny clusters of air sacs. It is here that the oxygen in the air is picked up and carried to all the cells in your body by your blood.

Just below your lungs is a muscle called the diaphragm [DIE-uh-FRAHM]. This muscle moves up and down to help you breathe.

⭢ **Learning Tip**

As you read, use your finger to trace the parts of the respiratory system on the diagram.

Getting Rid of Wastes

Your respiratory system has another job to do. Oxygen works with the nutrients in your cells to produce energy. Producing energy also produces water and carbon dioxide.

▲ Cells use oxygen and nutrients to produce energy. Water and carbon dioxide are also produced.

Water is very important to the cells in your body. Sometimes, however, your cells don't need all the water in your body. The water that is left over needs to be removed as waste. Some of the waste water is in the air you breathe out. This is why your breath is moist.

▶ What happens when you breathe on a mirror? What does this show you about your breath?

Carbon dioxide [KAR-buhn die-AWK-side] is a gas. It is harmful to your body, so your body must remove it quickly. Your blood picks up the carbon dioxide and takes it to your lungs. You get rid of it when you breathe out. Breathing out is called exhaling.

How You Breathe

The diaphragm helps the air move in and out of your lungs. When you breathe in, the diaphragm contracts and moves down. Muscles are attached to the ribs. These muscles lift your rib cage so it expands. When the rib cage expands, air enters the lungs. When you breathe out, the diaphragm relaxes and moves up. The muscles attached to your ribs also relax. When the rib cage gets smaller, air leaves the lungs.

⇨ Learning Tip

When you don't understand a word, you can often figure it out by reading the words around it. Read this paragraph. What do you think the word "contract" means?

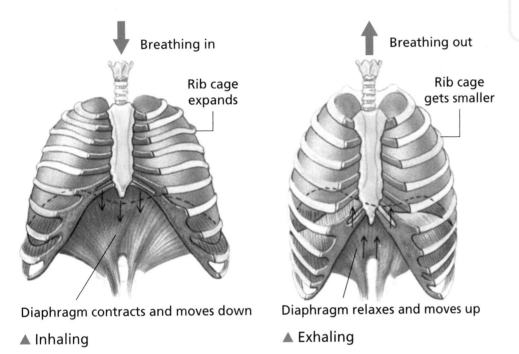

Breathing in

Rib cage expands

Diaphragm contracts and moves down

▲ Inhaling

Breathing out

Rib cage gets smaller

Diaphragm relaxes and moves up

▲ Exhaling

⇨ Check Your Understanding

1. Why does your body need oxygen? How does your body get this oxygen?

2. List two ways in which the air you breathe in is different from the air you breathe out.

3. Describe how air gets into and out of your body.

Chapter Review

Your body takes in nutrients and oxygen to keep you alive.

Key Idea: Your body is made of different systems, and each of these systems has a job to do.

Cell

Tissue

Organ

System

Vocabulary

cells p. 87

organs p. 87

Key Idea: Your digestive system breaks down food into nutrients.

Digestive system

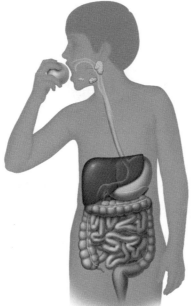

Vocabulary

digestion p. 88

nutrients p. 88

esophagus p. 89

stomach p. 89

small intestine
 p. 89

liver p. 89

large intestine
 p. 89

colon p. 89

FOOD

FOOD ENTERS BODY

DIGESTION

NUTRIENTS AND WATER ENTER CELLS

Key Idea: Your respiratory system takes in oxygen that your body uses to get energy from nutrients.

Vocabulary

oxygen p. 92

trachea p. 93

lung p. 93

carbon dioxide
  p. 94

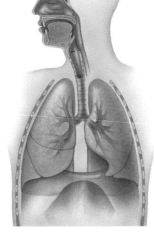

Respiratory system

Review Key Ideas and Vocabulary

Use the vocabulary words in your answers to the questions.

1. What three things make up every body system?

2. How are your respiratory and digestive systems related? Could you live with only one of these systems? Why or why not?

3. Explain how digestion happens in your mouth, stomach, and small intestine. You can use a table or a diagram in your answer.

4. Use each of the following words in a separate sentence: oxygen, carbon dioxide, water, lungs. Each sentence should explain the role of the substance or organ in your respiratory system.

Apply What You've Learned

Make a Good Health Poster

Looking Back

You have learned

- that your body needs both nutrients and oxygen to survive
- how your digestive system breaks down food into nutrients
- how your respiratory system takes in the oxygen your body needs to get energy from nutrients

In this activity, you will research how you can keep your digestive and respiratory systems healthy, so they can do their jobs. You will choose one of the ideas you researched to make a poster about staying healthy.

Demonstrate Your Learning

Plan and Make a Poster

1. Do research to find out how you can keep your digestive and respiratory systems healthy. Use different types of sources, such as books, magazines, videotapes, people, and the Internet.

2. Choose an idea for your poster. Here are three ideas:
   - Your body needs a variety of nutrients to stay healthy. The best way to get all these nutrients is to follow *Canada's Food Guide to Healthy Eating*. The Food Guide tells you the amount of food you need every day from each food group, depending on your age, activity level, and body size. If you follow the Food Guide, you will have a balanced diet. How could you convince people to follow the Food Guide?
   - Your body needs healthy lungs. Smoking causes lung cancer and other diseases of the respiratory system. How could you educate people about the dangers of smoking?
   - Exercise is a good way to keep your body healthy. Exercising on a regular basis allows your body to take in more oxygen. How could you encourage people to exercise?

3. When you have decided on an idea for your poster, think about how you could present the idea in words. Could you use your scientific knowledge to write a catchy saying or a short rhyme?

4. Brainstorm pictures you could find or draw for your poster. Your pictures should add to the message of your poster. Remember to ask your teacher's or parent's permission before cutting out any pictures from magazines.

5. Complete your poster, and display it for others to see.

⇨ Assessment Checklist

POSTER

As you plan and make your poster, make sure that you show you are able to

✔ explain the role of your digestive or respiratory system in keeping you healthy
✔ use appropriate scientific words
✔ communicate clearly in words and pictures

Your heart and blood carry nutrients and oxygen to your cells.

Key Ideas

▶ Your heart is a pump that pushes blood to all parts of your body.

▶ Blood carries oxygen to your cells and takes away carbon dioxide.

▶ Blood carries nutrients to your cells and takes away wastes.

▶ Your excretory system removes wastes from your blood.

▶ Your circulatory system interacts with other body systems to keep you healthy.

Put your hand over your heart. Can you feel your heart beating? If you are sitting quietly in a chair, your heart may be beating so softly that you feel no heartbeat at all. Now look at the photo. How hard do you think these runners' hearts are beating? Why does your heart beat faster and harder when you are active? Why does your heart beat at all?

In this chapter, you will learn how your heart and blood keep you healthy. You will discover that your blood carries everything your cells need to do their special jobs, such as providing energy for running.

Your Body's Transportation System

Your body takes in nutrients and oxygen that your cells need to stay alive and healthy. The job of carrying nutrients and oxygen to all the cells in your body is done by your circulatory [SUR-kyuh-luh-TOR-ee] system. Your circulatory system is made up of your heart, blood vessels, and blood.

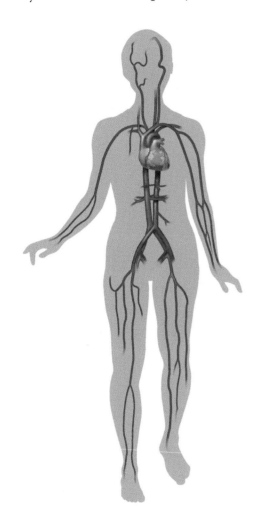

◄ Your circulatory system is like a huge transportation system. It moves nutrients and oxygen to your cells and takes away wastes produced by your cells. It also defends your body against diseases.

⇨ Check Your Understanding

1. What are the main organs in the circulatory system?

2. How is your circulatory system like a transportation system?

2   *The Job of Your Heart*

When you think of a heart, do you think of the heart shape used on Valentine's Day cards? Your heart doesn't look anything like that.

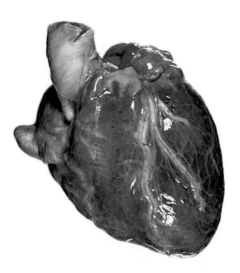

◄ Your heart is about the size of an adult's fist.

⇨ Learning Tip

Connect this information to your own body. Place your hand over your heart to feel it beating. Try to picture your heart contracting and then relaxing.

Your **heart** is a pump. Its job is to push your blood so that your blood keeps moving through your body all the time.

Your heart pumps about 70 times each minute. It does this every single minute, for your whole life. The pumping is actually your heart contracting and then relaxing. When your heart contracts, it tightens up. Each time it contracts, it pushes blood. This is called a heartbeat. You can feel your heartbeat by feeling your **pulse.** Each time your heart contracts, it produces a pulse. So you can measure the number of times your heart beats by feeling your pulse.

Did you know?

As a rule, the bigger the animal, the slower its heart beats. A blue whale's heart, for example, beats about 7 times each minute. A mouse's heart, on the other hand, beats about 600 times a minute.

Try This

Work Like Your Heart

Skills Focus: observing, measuring, inferring

1. Work with a partner. Hold a soft ball, such as a rubber ball, in one of your hands. Imagine that it is your heart.

2. Squeeze the ball tightly, and then relax your hand. This is one heartbeat. Do this as many times as you can in a minute. Count the number of times. Your partner will tell you when a minute is up.

3. Change roles, and have your partner squeeze the ball.

4. How many times were you able to squeeze the ball? How many times does your heart contract in a minute? Can you squeeze the ball as quickly as your heart contracts? Try it.

5. Does your heart work hard? How do you know?

How Your Heart Works

Your heart has a right side and a left side. The right side of your heart receives blood from your body. The blood is carrying a lot of carbon dioxide. Your heart sends the blood to your lungs. In your lungs, the blood gives up the carbon dioxide it is carrying and picks up oxygen. The blood now goes into the left side of your heart and is pumped out to the rest of your body. The blood delivers the oxygen to your cells and picks up carbon dioxide. Then it returns to the right side of your heart.

Examine this diagram to see the path of blood as it moves through your body.

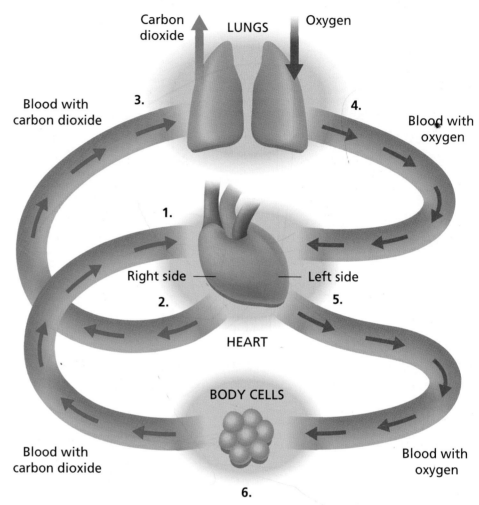

1. Blood with carbon dioxide goes into the right side of your heart.

2. Your heart pumps the blood with carbon dioxide to your lungs.

3. Your lungs exhale the carbon dioxide and inhale oxygen.

4. Blood with oxygen goes from your lungs to the left side of your heart.

5. Your heart pumps the blood with oxygen throughout your body.

6. The cells in your body take the oxygen from the blood and put carbon dioxide into the blood.

How Your Blood Travels

How does your blood get to where it's going? It travels through blood vessels. **Blood vessels** are hollow tubes that contain your blood. Your blood moves through your body in these blood vessels. Two types of blood vessels are arteries [AHR-tuh-REEZ] and veins [VAYNZ].

Arteries are thick blood vessels that carry blood away from your heart. Almost all the blood they carry is full of oxygen. This oxygen is passed into the cells of the body.

Veins are blood vessels that carry blood back to the heart. Almost all the blood they carry has very little oxygen, but a lot of carbon dioxide. The carbon dioxide is passed into the lungs, where it is exhaled.

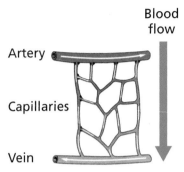

▲ Tiny capillaries connect your veins and arteries.

Arteries and veins are connected to each other through tiny blood vessels called capillaries [kuh-PILL-uh-reez]. Oxygen and nutrients are passed from the arteries, through the capillaries, and into your body cells. Wastes, such as carbon dioxide, are passed from your body cells, through the capillaries, and into the veins.

Look at the diagram of the circulatory system on page 101. The red blood vessels show blood that is carrying oxygen. The blue blood vessels show blood that has little oxygen, but a lot of carbon dioxide. Which of these blood vessels are arteries? Which are veins?

⇨ Check Your Understanding

1. What does your pulse tell you?
2. Where does the blood from the right side of your heart go? What is this blood carrying?
3. Where does the blood from the left side of your heart go? What is this blood carrying?
4. How are arteries and veins the same? How are they different?

Your Blood and What It Does

You probably think of blood as a liquid. But blood is actually made up of two parts: a liquid part and a solid part. The liquid part, called plasma [PLAHZ-muh], is mostly water. The solid part is made up of **blood cells.** There are three kinds of blood cells.

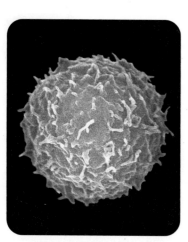

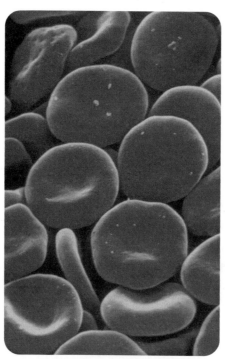

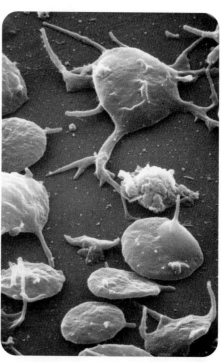

▲ White blood cells are larger than red blood cells. They protect your body from harmful substances that enter your body and can make you sick.

▲ Red blood cells carry oxygen to all parts of your body. They give your blood its red colour. Red blood cells make up nearly all of your blood cells (99%).

▲ Platelets are much smaller than red blood cells. They form a plug, called a clot, that stops you from bleeding. White blood cells and platelets make up a small number of your blood cells (1%).

The Job of Your Blood

Red blood cells pick up oxygen in your lungs. The oxygen moves into each red blood cell through its cell membrane. The cell **membrane** is the outer part of the cell. It lets needed materials enter the cell. It also lets wastes move out of the cell. All the cells in your body have a cell membrane.

Each red blood cell then travels in the plasma to a cell in your body, and passes oxygen to this cell. The body cell passes some carbon dioxide into the red blood cell. Most of the carbon dioxide is passed into the plasma. Your blood continues on its way, taking the carbon dioxide back to the lungs, where you breathe it out.

The plasma in your blood carries nutrients, including water, from your digestive system to your body cells. The nutrients pass into your body cells the same way that oxygen does.

As your body cells use the nutrients, they produce wastes. The plasma carries away these wastes and passes them to special organs that remove them from your body.

Learning Tip

After you read each paragraph on this page, ask yourself questions to check your understanding: What did I just read? What did it mean? If the ideas aren't clear to you, reread the paragraph.

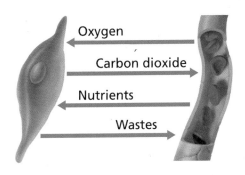

◄ Red blood cells take oxygen to your cells. Plasma carries nutrients to your cells and takes away carbon dioxide and wastes.

Your blood also carries messenger chemicals, called hormones. Hormones carry many different kinds of messages to different body systems. For example, when you see something scary, a hormone makes your heart beat faster, causes you to sweat, and makes your muscles contract. These changes prepare your body to deal with the scary situation. When the scary situation is over, your body returns to normal.

Check Your Understanding

1. What are the three kinds of blood cells that make up the solid part of your blood? What is the main job of each kind of blood cell?

2. How do oxygen and carbon dioxide move into and out of cells?

3. What does your blood transport, besides oxygen and carbon dioxide?

4 Design Your Own Experiment

○ SKILLS MENU

○ Questioning	● Measuring
● Predicting	○ Classifying
● Designing Experiments	○ Inferring
	● Interpreting Data
● Fair Testing	
● Observing	● Communicating

Does Exercise Affect Your Heart Rate?

Your heart rate is the number of times your heart beats in one minute. You can measure your heart rate by counting your pulse. Place two fingers of your right hand on the inside of your left wrist. Press and move your fingers about until you feel your pulse.

Work with a partner to design and carry out an experiment to find out if your heart rate changes when you exercise.

Question

Does exercise affect your heart rate?

Prediction

Make a prediction about whether exercise will have an effect on your heart rate. If you think it will have an effect, make a prediction about the kind of effect it will have.

Materials

Decide what materials you will need for your experiment. Check with your teacher to make sure that these materials are safe for you to use.

> ↪ **Learning Tip**
>
> Before you begin this experiment, review Design Your Own Experiment in the Skills Handbook.

 Do not do the exercising part of this experiment if you are not allowed to participate in gym class.

> ° **Procedure**
>
> Design a procedure to test your prediction. A procedure is a step-by-step description of how you will conduct your experiment. It must be clear enough for someone else to follow and do the same experiment.

Think about questions like these:
- How will you measure heart rate?
- Will you measure heart rate before exercising?
- What type of exercise will you do? How long will you exercise?
- Will you measure heart rate after exercising? How long after?
- Will you do more than one trial?

Hand in your procedure, including any safety precautions, to your teacher for approval.

Data and Observations

Create a data table to record your observations. Record your observations as you carry out your experiment.

Interpret Data and Observations

1. Did your heart rate change when you exercised? How did it change?

2. Look back at your predictions. Did your results fully support, partly support, or not support your predictions? Write a conclusion for your experiment.

3. What happened to your heart rate after you stopped exercising? Why do you think this happened?

Apply and Extend

1. What do you think would happen to your heart rate if you exercised for twice as long? Make a prediction, and then test your prediction to see if you were correct.

⇨ Check Your Understanding

1. What variable did you change in your experiment?
2. What variable did you measure?

Getting Rid of Wastes Through Your Blood

Your body gets rid of wastes in many ways. Your blood takes carbon dioxide to your lungs, where it is exhaled. Some water is also exhaled. Your large intestine gets rid of solid wastes that remain after digestion.

When your cells use oxygen to produce energy, they also produce wastes. These wastes move from your cells to your blood. Your body gets rid of these wastes in the following two ways:

1. As sweat: The water that leaves your body through your skin contains waste salts. This is why you can sometimes taste salt on your skin after you have exercised.

2. Through your excretory [EK-skrih-TOR-ee] system: This system is made up of two kidneys and a bladder.

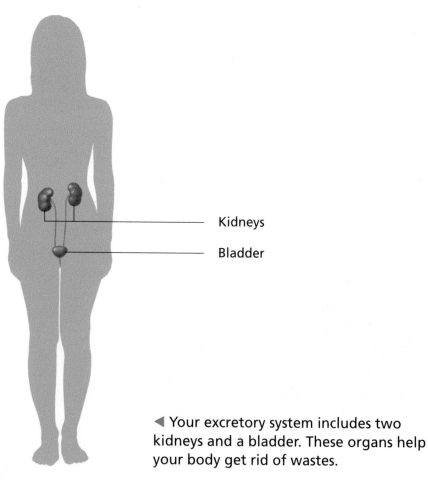

Kidneys

Bladder

◄ Your excretory system includes two kidneys and a bladder. These organs help your body get rid of wastes.

Filtering Your Blood

Kidneys are organs that filter blood. About 180 L (litres) of blood pass through your kidneys every day. Your kidneys filter out the wastes from the blood. They return the nutrients that your body needs and most of the water back to the blood.

Some wastes and water form urine [YOOR-in]. Urine is sent to the bladder. The **bladder** is a balloon-like organ that stretches to hold the urine until it is released from your body.

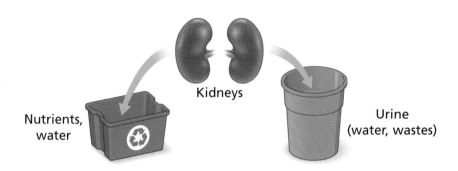

Nutrients, water

Kidneys

Urine (water, wastes)

◄ Your excretory system removes some substances from your body and recycles other substances.

Your kidneys have another important job. They help to balance the amount of water in your body. You need just the right amount of water—too much or too little can be dangerous. If you have too much water in your body, your kidneys will put less water back into the blood and more water in the urine. If you have too little water in your body, your kidneys will put more water back into the blood and less water in the urine.

⇨ Check Your Understanding

1. How does your body get rid of wastes in your blood?
2. What substances do your kidneys leave in your blood? What substances do they filter out?
3. How are your kidneys and the amount of water in your body connected?
4. What would happen to your blood if your kidneys stopped working?

How Your Circulatory System Interacts with Other Body Systems

▲ Each system in your body has its own important job to do. But each system also works with all the other systems to keep you healthy.

You have now learned about the digestive, respiratory, circulatory, and excretory systems. You have also learned how these systems are connected. Here are four examples:

- Your digestive system breaks down food into nutrients. Your circulatory system carries these nutrients to all your body cells.
- Your respiratory system brings in oxygen. Your circulatory system carries the oxygen to all your body cells.
- Your circulatory system picks up carbon dioxide from your body cells. Your respiratory system gets rid of the carbon dioxide.
- Your circulatory system picks up wastes from your body cells. Your excretory system gets rid of the wastes.

Look at the diagram on the next page. Follow the arrows to see how the four systems are connected.

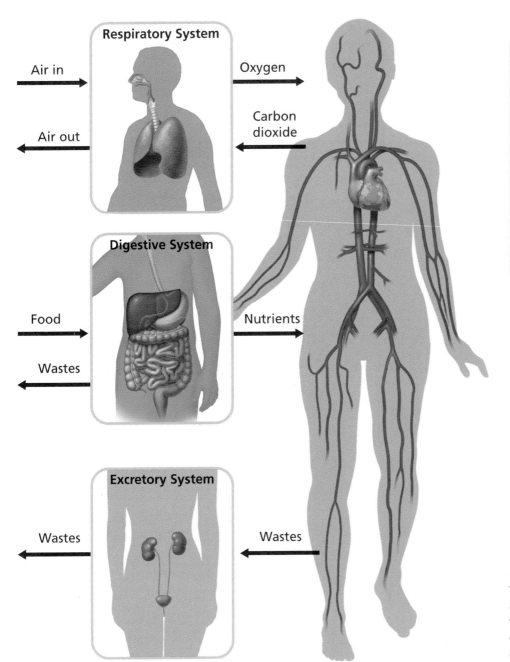

Respiratory System

Air in

Air out

Oxygen

Carbon dioxide

Digestive System

Food

Wastes

Nutrients

Excretory System

Wastes

Wastes

⇨ Learning Tip

To read the diagram, follow the direction of the arrows. Look at the arrow at the top on the left. Read the label. What does this tell you? Now look at the arrow to the right and read the label. What does this tell you? Do the same for the rest of the arrows.

◀ **Circulatory System**
The circulatory system brings oxygen and nutrients to all the cells in the body and carries away carbon dioxide and wastes.

⇨ Check Your Understanding

1. How is the digestive system connected to the circulatory system?

2. How is the respiratory system connected to the circulatory system?

3. How does the excretory system help the circulatory system do its job?

5 Chapter Review

Your heart and blood carry nutrients and oxygen to your cells.

Key Idea: Your heart is a pump that pushes blood to all parts of your body.

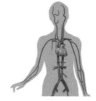

Circulatory system

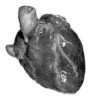

Human heart

Vocabulary

heart p. 102

pulse p. 102

Key Idea: Blood carries oxygen to your cells and takes away carbon dioxide.

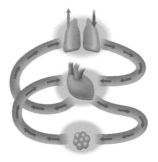

Vocabulary

blood vessels
 p. 105

arteries p. 105

veins p. 105

blood cells p. 106

membrane p. 106

Key Idea: Blood carries nutrients to your cells and takes away wastes.

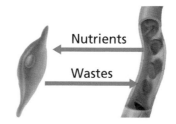

Nutrients

Wastes

Key Idea: Your excretory system removes wastes from your blood.

Excretory system

Vocabulary

kidneys p. 111

bladder p. 111

Key Idea: Your circulatory system interacts with other body systems to keep you healthy.

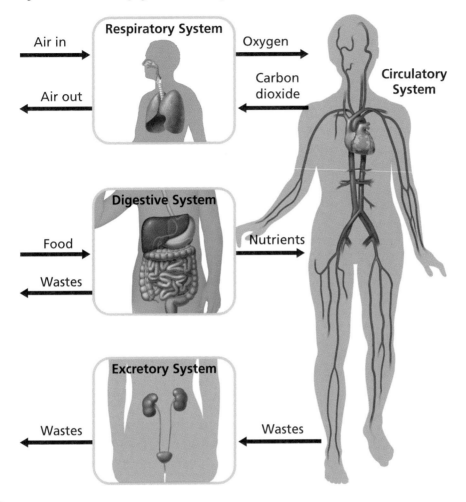

Respiratory System
Air in
Air out
Oxygen
Carbon dioxide

Circulatory System

Digestive System
Food
Wastes
Nutrients

Excretory System
Wastes
Wastes

Review Key Ideas and Vocabulary

Use the vocabulary words in your answers to the questions.

1. How is your blood able to bring some materials to your cells and remove other materials?

2. Explain what happens as your blood travels to and from your heart. Include a labelled diagram with your explanation.

3. Describe how your kidneys and bladder get rid of wastes.

4. How do the circulatory system, the respiratory system, the digestive system, and the excretory system work together?

Visit the Quiz Centre at: www·science·nelson·com GO

Apply What You've Learned

Write a Story about the Path of Blood in the Body

Looking Back

You have learned

- how your heart pumps blood throughout your body
- how your blood carries oxygen and nutrients to your cells and takes away carbon dioxide and other wastes
- how blood passes through your excretory system, where wastes are removed from your body

In this activity, you will create a picture book story describing the path that blood takes as it travels in the body.

Demonstrate Your Learning

Plan a Picture Book

1. Work with a group to review the path that blood takes as it travels through the lungs, heart, and body, and back to the lungs. Make a list of the different parts of the body it visits. Your list should
   - start with the blood leaving the lungs and heading for the heart
   - describe the other parts of the body it visits
   - describe what it picks up and drops off at each different part of the body

2. Plan a picture book story that describes the path of blood to read to younger students. Your plan should
   - follow the list you made
   - describe what the blood does in each part of the body
   - explain what you will write on each page of your picture book, and describe the pictures you will use

Create a Picture Book

1. Decide who will do the different tasks to create your picture book. For example, will each person in the group do one page of the book, or will some people do all the writing and others do all the pictures?

2. Complete your picture book, and read it to students in a lower grade.

⇨ Assessment Checklist

PLAN

As you plan your picture book, make sure that you show you are able to

✔ accurately describe, in words and pictures, the path that blood takes and what it does in each part of the body
✔ use appropriate scientific words
✔ communicate clearly and make decisions that everyone in the group agrees with

CREATE

As you create your picture book, make sure that you show you are able to

✔ work cooperatively with other students by sharing tasks

Chapter 6

Your bones, muscles, and skin support and protect your body.

Key Ideas

▸ Your bones give your body support and shape, and protect your organs.

▸ Your bones and muscles make it possible for you to move.

▸ Your skin covers and protects your body.

▸ Your bones, muscles, and skin interact with other body systems to keep you healthy.

Think of all the ways you move in a day. You lift your arm to reach for something, you chew and swallow your food, you bend over to tie your shoe. Maybe you run, swim, or throw a ball. What makes it possible for you to move in so many different ways?

In this chapter, you will discover how your bones and muscles allow you to move. You will learn how your bones, muscles, and skin protect and support all the other systems in your body. You will also learn how your bones, muscles, and skin help to keep you healthy.

Your Body's Framework

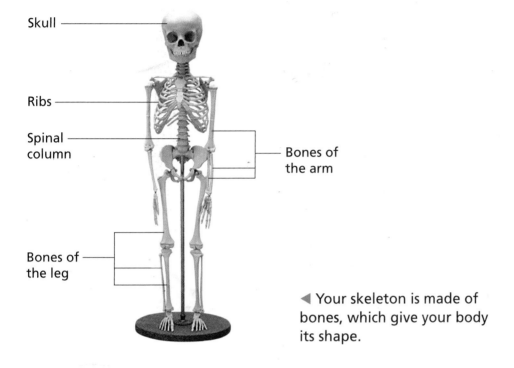

Skull

Ribs

Spinal
column

Bones of
the arm

Bones of
the leg

◀ Your skeleton is made of
bones, which give your body
its shape.

What would you look like if you didn't have any bones?
You would look like a blob on the floor! Your **bones** form
a skeleton [SKEL-uh-tuhn] that gives shape to your body and
supports it. Your skeleton also protects your internal organs,
such as your heart and your lungs.

Each bone is made of different groups of living cells.
Each cell takes in nutrients and sends out wastes, just like
every other cell in your body. Bones store minerals, such as
calcium [KAL-see-uhm], which help to keep them hard
and strong. This is why bones do not easily break. If they
do break, they can heal.

⇨ Check Your Understanding

1. What makes your bones so important?
2. Why do we know bones are alive?

2 Your Bones

⇨ **Learning Tip**

Preview the section and read the headings. What types of bones will you be learning about in this section?

Each bone in your body does a different job for you. Your skull, spinal column, and ribs, and the bones of your arms and legs are different shapes because they do different jobs.

Your Skull

Your skull is important because it protects your brain, which is very soft. It also gives your face its shape.

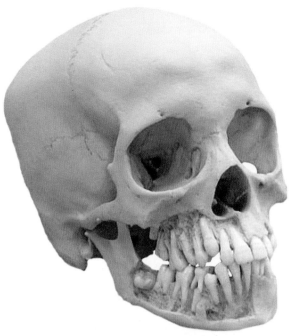

▲ Your skull is made up of 28 bones. The largest bone is the bone that surrounds your brain. Other bones form your face.

Your Spinal Column

Attached to the base of your skull is your spinal column. Your spinal column is sometimes called your backbone. It is made of bones that are stacked, one on top of each other.

Your spinal column supports your head and body. Muscles are attached to the bones in your spinal column. Your spinal column works with your muscles to let you move your head and bend and twist your body.

▲ Your spinal column lets you bend over to do things like touch your toes.

Your Ribs

Your ribs are 12 pairs of flat bones that are shaped like a cage. Your rib cage protects your heart and lungs. Your rib cage is involved in breathing, as well. Muscles are attached to your ribs. When you inhale, these muscles contract to lift your rib cage so that your lungs can expand. When you exhale, your rib cage muscles relax. Your rib cage gets smaller and the air leaves your lungs.

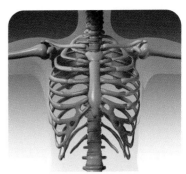

▲ Your ribs are shaped like a cage, to protect your heart and lungs.

The Bones in Your Arms and Legs

Each of your arms has one long bone that runs from the shoulder to the elbow and two long bones that run from the elbow to the wrist bones. Your hand bones are attached to the wrist bones.

Each of your legs has one long bone that attaches to the hip and goes to the knee. Two bones run from the knee to the anklebones. Attached to the anklebones are your foot bones.

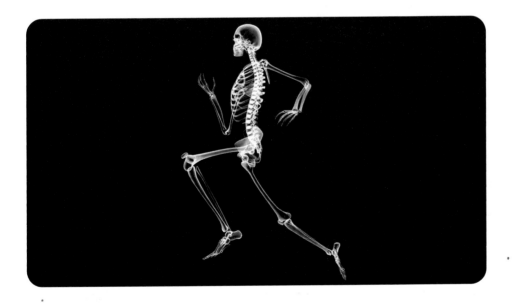

◀ The bones in the arms and legs bend and move so we can run, jump, and move in many ways.

⇨ Check Your Understanding

1. Name four groups of bones. Explain what each group of bones does.

3 How Your Bones Move

Your bones would not be able to move the way they do if you didn't have joints. A joint is formed where two bones meet.

How Your Joints Work

Some joints, like most of the joints in your skull, allow little or no movement. Other joints allow the bones to move. At these movable joints, the bones are just far enough away from each other to allow them to move. Movable joints are found in many places in your body. How many can you find? Can you find 10 … 20 … 50 … 100?

Explore Your Movable Joints

Skills Focus: observing, communicating

1. Find five places in your body where there are movable joints. Explore how these joints move.

2. In your notebook, make a table like the one below to record your observations. An example has been done for you.

		Movable Joints	
Joint	What is the joint called?	What two bones meet at the joint?	How does the joint move?
1	elbow	upper arm bone and lower arm bone	back and forth; up and down
2			

Ligaments [LIG-uh-muhnts] are strong, elastic groups of cells that stretch and tighten, like rubber bands. They hold the bones of the movable joints together.

The Role of Cartilage

Without protection, the bones at your joints would rub together and wear away over time. This is why the ends of these bones are covered by pads of cartilage [KAR-tuh-lihj]. **Cartilage** is a layer of cells in a gel-like material. Cartilage reduces friction between the ends of the bones at your joints. It also acts like a cushion for your joints when you jump.

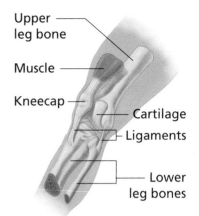

Upper leg bone

Muscle

Kneecap

Cartilage

Ligaments

Lower leg bones

▲ Ligaments hold the upper and lower leg bones together at the knee joint. A thin layer of cartilage at the ends of the bones stops the bones from rubbing together.

Did you know?

You have cartilage in other places, besides your bones. Your ears and the end of your nose are made of cartilage. What would these structures be like if they were made of bone instead of cartilage?

Bone Marrow

Your bones have another very important job. The insides of many bones contain marrow. Some of the marrow is red. The red marrow produces the blood cells that make up a large part of your blood. In children, large bones, such as your ribs and the bones in your legs, make blood cells in their marrow.

⇨ Check Your Understanding

1. Name two joints in your body that move in different ways. Describe how they move.

2. How do ligaments help your skeleton and body move?

3. How does cartilage help when you are running and jumping?

4. What important role does bone marrow play in your body?

Chapter 6

4 Conduct an Investigation

○ SKILLS MENU

○ Questioning	● Measuring
● Predicting	○ Classifying
○ Designing Experiments	○ Inferring
● Fair Testing	● Interpreting Data
● Observing	● Communicating

chicken bones   vinegar

jars

water

permanent marker   masking tape

triple beam balance

 Make sure you wash your hands with soap and water after handling the chicken bones. Be careful when using glass containers.

The Role of Calcium in Bones

Calcium from the food you eat settles in the outer parts of your bones. Calcium helps to keep your bones hard and strong. What would happen if the calcium left your bones or if you didn't get enough calcium in your food?

In this investigation, you will use vinegar to eat away the calcium in a bone. This will show what happens to bones when calcium is removed.

Question

What happens to bones that lose calcium?

Prediction

Make a prediction about how bones change when calcium is removed from them.

Materials

- 2 small chicken leg bones
- white vinegar
- 2 labelled jars
- water in a plastic jug
- permanent marker
- masking tape
- triple beam balance

○ Procedure

Step 1 Work with a partner. Copy the following table into your notebook.

Data Table for Investigation 6.4		
Day	Container 1 (bone 1)	Container 2 (bone 2)
1		
2		

124

NEL

Step 2 Your teacher will give you two bones. Label them 1 and 2 with a permanent marker. Try to bend the bones to see how flexible they are. Weigh the bones. Carefully examine them. Write all your observations and measurements in your table (day 1).

Step 3 Place bone 1 in container 1. Add water until the bone is covered.

Step 4 Place bone 2 in container 2. Add vinegar until the bone is covered.

Step 5 After one day, take the bones out of the containers. Before handling the bones in vinegar, empty the vinegar into a sink and run fresh water over the bones. Check for flexibility and weigh the bones. Record your observations and measurements (day 2).

Step 6 Put fresh vinegar and water in the two containers. Put the bones back in the correct containers.

Step 7 Continue doing this for three more days.

Interpret Data and Observations

1. Use your observations and measurements to compare the two bones. What happened to the bone in the vinegar? What happened to the bone in the water?

2. Was your prediction correct?

Apply and Extend

1. What do think would happen if your bones did not get enough calcium every day?

Check Your Understanding

1. Why did you have a chicken bone in water in this investigation? How did it help you understand what happens to a bone if calcium is removed?

2. Was this investigation a fair test? Why or why not?

5 Your Muscular System

Your bones cannot move by themselves. They need muscles [MUSS-uhlz] to make them move. In fact, muscles cause every movement you make. **Muscles** are tissues that are attached to bones. They are attached by strong, elastic bands of cells called **tendons** [TEN-duhnz]. Tendons are similar to ligaments, but they attach muscles to bones instead of bones to bones, like ligaments.

Muscles work by contracting. When they contract, they pull on the bones they are attached to. When you want your bones to move, your muscles will react to make this happen. For example, if you want to kick a ball, one group of muscles will contract to lift your foot, and another group of muscles will bend your knee. Then other groups of muscles will contract to straighten your leg and foot to kick the ball.

▲ Can you find the muscles the girl is using to kick the ball?

Did you know?

You have over 600 muscles in your body. Your muscles make up nearly half of the mass of your body.

Voluntary Muscles

Some muscles, such as the muscles you use to kick a ball, do their job because you want them to. These muscles are called voluntary [VOL-uhn-TEHR-ee] muscles.

Voluntary muscles work in pairs to make your body move. Put one of your arms straight out in front of you, with the palm of your hand up. Bend your arm toward you, and feel the muscle in the inside of your upper arm. This is your bicep [BY-sehp] muscle. Now hold the back of your upper arm above the elbow and straighten your arm. You will feel your tricep [TRY-sehp] muscles. Bicep and tricep muscles work together to bend and straighten your arm.

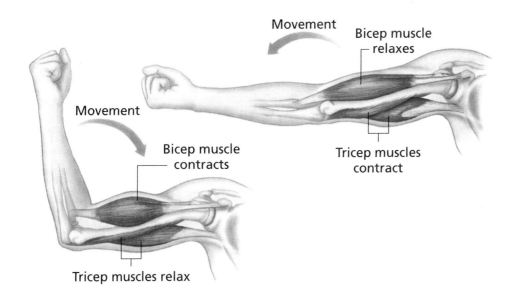

Movement

Bicep muscle relaxes

Movement

Bicep muscle contracts

Tricep muscles contract

Tricep muscles relax

◀ To bend your arm at your elbow, the bicep muscle contracts and the tricep muscles relax. To straighten your arm, the tricep muscles contract and the bicep muscle relaxes.

Involuntary Muscles

There are many muscles that work without you thinking about what is happening. These muscles are called involuntary [in-VOL-uhn-TEHR-ee] muscles.

For example, you have muscles that move the food through your digestive system. These muscles contract and relax slowly to push the food along. Your heart is made of a special type of involuntary muscle. It will beat faster or slower automatically, depending on what you are doing. Your diaphragm is also an involuntary muscle. It controls your breathing.

Try This

Identify the Type of Muscle

Skills Focus: observing, inferring

1. Work with a partner. Look in a mirror for one minute. Have your partner count the number of times your eyes close automatically. Record the number.

2. Stare in the mirror for as long as you can without closing your eyes. Have your partner time you. Record the time.

3. Switch roles with your partner.

4. Which type of muscles do your eyelids have? How do you know?

5. Can you control some involuntary muscles? How do you know?

6. Why is it important for some muscles to work automatically?

Did you know?

The human face has many small muscles. When you frown, you use 34 muscles. When you smile, you only use 13 muscles. It is much easier to smile than to frown!

Learning Tip

Look back through the section to find the answers to these questions. Do not guess. Even if you remember the answer, it is a good idea to go back and check it.

Check Your Understanding

1. How do muscles move bones?

2. What are tendons? How are they the same as ligaments? How are they different from ligaments?

3. What two types of muscles do you have? Which type do you use when you throw a ball?

4. What happens to the muscles in your upper arm when you bend your arm at the elbow?

Tech·CONNECT

Computer Muscle

Imagine a computer that could read your mind. If you wanted to send an e-mail, you wouldn't need a keyboard and a mouse. You could just think about what you wanted to say, and the computer would take care of the rest. This might sound like science fiction, but it may be closer to reality than you think.

Muscles can become paralyzed [PEHR-uh-LIZD] because of an injury or illness. When muscles are paralyzed, they cannot move the part of the body they are attached to. People who are paralyzed are unable to move their legs or arms, or both. Now scientists have a new tool that may help these people do some everyday things.

Scientists have implanted a tiny computer chip into the brain of a man named Matt who is paralyzed from his neck down. The chip reads Matt's thoughts and sends them to a computer through tiny wires that are attached to his head. The computer then performs the action that Matt thought about. For example, if Matt wants to turn on a television or change the channel, he thinks the thought and the computer sends the command to the television.

Similarly, Matt can send his thoughts to a robotic arm and make its hand open and close. He can also move the robotic arm and make it pick up and drop objects.

▲ A computer chip in Matt's brain lets him send his thoughts to a computer to perform the action.

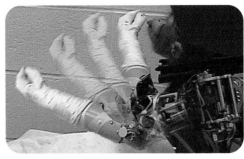

▲ This chimpanzee's thoughts are controlling the robotic arm. Matt uses a similar arm.

Scientists hope that a computer chip can eventually be used to help people who are paralyzed move again. They want to find a way to send messages from a computer chip in the brain to paralyzed arms and legs so that people can move them just by thinking about it.

Skin: Your Protective Covering

It is not just your bones and muscles that support and protect your body. Your skin also does this. Your **skin** is the largest organ in your body. It provides you with a waterproof cover, and holds all the systems in your body safely inside. As well, it helps to prevent infections from entering your body. Infections can enter your body if you have a cut or scrape on your skin.

Your skin has different layers. The top layer is where new skin cells are made. They are made at the bottom of the top layer and move to the surface of your skin. By the time they get to the surface, they are dead. Then they flake off. In fact, you lose 30 000 to 40 000 dead skin cells every minute of every day. By doing this, your skin is always replacing itself so that it can protect you better.

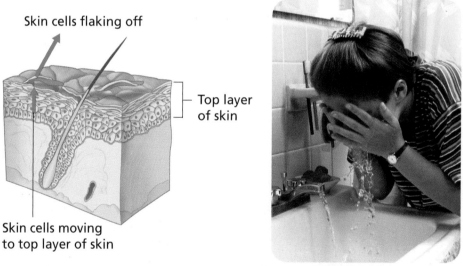

Skin cells flaking off

Top layer of skin

Skin cells moving to top layer of skin

▲ It is important to wash your skin to remove dead skin cells and dirt.

Did you know that your nails and your hair are part of your skin? They grow from one of the lower layers. Both your nails and your hair protect your body. It's easy to see how your nails protect the ends of your fingers and toes, but how does your hair protect you?

You have hair on nearly every part of the outside of your body. Some places that do not have hair are your lips, the palms of your hands, and the soles of your feet. The hair on your head helps to keep your head warm and protects your skull, like a cushion. Your eyebrows protect your eyes from sweat that could drip into them. Your eyelashes help to stop things such as dust from getting in your eyes.

Did you know?

You will grow about 15 m of fingernails in your lifetime. You will also grow about 1 km of hair.

Try This | Compare Fingerprints

Skills Focus: observing

Each person has unique skin patterns on their fingers called fingerprints. Your fingerprints mark you as different from every other person in the world. This is why fingerprints are used to identify people.

1. Rub a pencil on a piece of paper until you have a dark smudge, about 2 cm by 2 cm.

2. Rub the tip of your left index finger on the pencil smudge until it is covered with the pencil lead.

3. Place a strip of clear tape over your fingertip lengthwise. Press down gently on the tape.

4. Carefully remove the tape, and stick it on a piece of white paper.

5. Use a magnifying glass to examine your fingerprint. Compare your fingerprint with other students' fingerprints. Are they all different?

⇨ Check Your Understanding

1. What are two important jobs of your skin?

2. How does your skin keep itself new? Why do you think this is important?

How Your Bones, Muscles, and Skin Interact with Other Body Systems

Your bones, muscles, and skin all have important jobs in supporting, protecting, and moving your body.

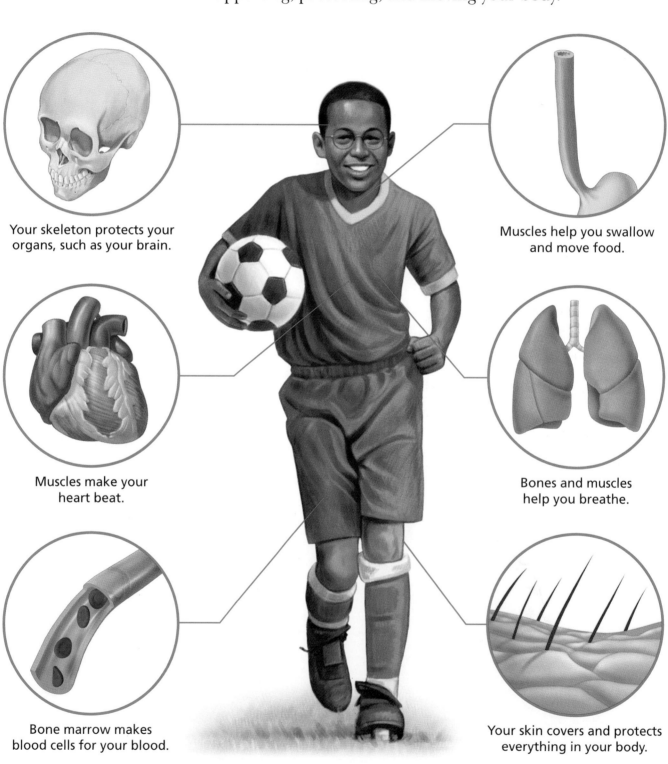

Your skeleton protects your organs, such as your brain.

Muscles help you swallow and move food.

Muscles make your heart beat.

Bones and muscles help you breathe.

Bone marrow makes blood cells for your blood.

Your skin covers and protects everything in your body.

Your other body systems help your bones, muscles, and skin do their jobs.

- Your digestive system provides the nutrients that the cells in your bones, muscles, and skin need in order to grow and repair themselves.
- Your respiratory system provides oxygen to keep the cells in your bones, muscles, and skin healthy and growing.
- Your circulatory system carries nutrients and oxygen to the cells in your bones, muscles, and skin. It also carries wastes away from these cells.

⇨ Learning Tip

This page describes how your digestive, respiratory, and circulatory systems help your bones, muscles, and skin do their jobs. Before you read, write three questions that you should be able to answer after reading.

⇨ Check Your Understanding

1. • Write the following words in circles on a page in your notebook:
   - digestive system
   - respiratory system
   - circulatory system
   - muscular system
   - skeletal system
   - skin

   • Draw a line from the digestive system to any other circle it is connected to. On the line, write how the two circles are connected. Do the same for the other circles. You only need to have one line from each circle, but you might want to have more.

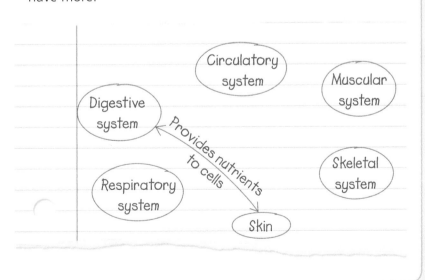

Chapter Review

Your bones, muscles, and skin support and protect your body.

Key Idea: Your bones give your body support and shape, and protect your organs.

Skeletal system

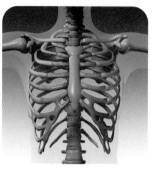

Rib cage

Vocabulary

bones p. 119

Key Idea: Your bones and muscles make it possible for you to move.

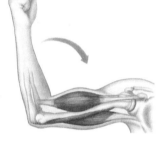

Vocabulary

ligaments p. 122
cartilage p. 123
muscles p. 126
tendons p. 126

Key Idea: Your skin covers and protects your body.

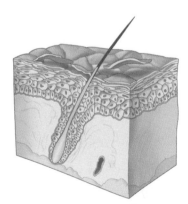

Vocabulary

skin p. 130

Key Idea: Your bones, muscles, and skin interact with other body systems to keep you healthy.

Review Key Ideas and Vocabulary

Use the vocabulary words in your answers to the questions.

1. What are the jobs of the skeletal system?

2. How do the skeletal and muscular systems work together?

3. Where do you find cartilage in your body?

4. What is the difference between voluntary and involuntary muscles?

5. Name one job that skin has. How does this job help your body?

6. Describe two ways that your skeletal system interacts with your other body systems.

7. Describe two ways that your muscular system interacts with your other body systems.

Apply What You've Learned

Design and Build a Model Leg

Looking Back

You have learned

- that some bones come together at movable joints
- that bones at movable joints are attached to each other with ligaments
- that muscles are attached to bones with tendons
- how your bones and muscles work together

In this activity, you will design and build a model of a leg to show what you have learned about how your skeleton moves.

Demonstrate Your Learning

Design and Build a Model Leg

1. Work with a partner to design a model of a leg. Your model leg should include

  - the upper leg
  - the knee joint
  - the lower leg
  - the ankle joint
  - the foot (You do not have to include the toes.)

  When your model leg is complete, you should be able to move it to show how it could kick a ball.

2. Draw a design for your model leg. Plan which materials you will use for the bones, muscles, ligaments, and tendons. For example, you could use cardboard, rubber bands, art straws, string, tape, scissors, brass paper fasteners, and a one-hole punch. You could also use other materials that are available in your classroom or your home, such as deflated balloons, paper tubes, stuffed socks, straightened paper clips, corks, Styrofoam, half a tennis ball, wood, plastic tubing, pipe cleaners, craft sticks, and hinges.

   Label your design to identify the materials you will use and the parts of the leg.

3. Show your design to your teacher. Once you have your teacher's approval, build your model.

Communicate

1. Present your model to your class. Demonstrate how the bones, joints, muscles, ligaments, and tendons work together to kick a ball. In your demonstration, point out each of these parts, and explain what each one is doing.

> ## ⇨ Assessment Checklist
>
> ### MODEL LEG
> **As you design and build your model leg, make sure that you show you are able to**
>
> ✔ model accurately the bones, joints, muscles, ligaments, and tendons in a human leg
> ✔ demonstrate how the bones and muscles in the leg and foot work together to help you move
> ✔ use scientific words correctly in your demonstration
> ✔ work cooperatively with another student

Your nervous system controls all your other body systems.

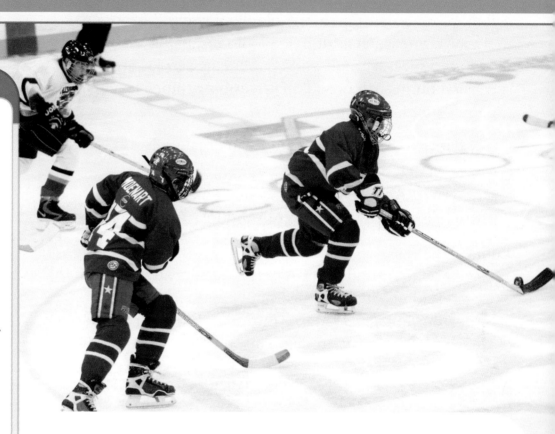

Key Ideas

- Your brain is the control centre of your body.

- Nerves send messages to and from your brain to all parts of your body.

- Your sense organs react to touch, smell, taste, sight, and sound.

- Your nervous system is connected to all the other systems in your body.

Hockey players have a lot to think about. As they race around the rink on skates, they have to keep track of every movement and sound around them. They have to decide, in a split second, what to do next.

Like a hockey player, you are taking in information and reacting to it all the time. You hear your name, and you turn toward the sound. You trip and put your arms out to stop yourself. What is making you react the way you do to these things?

In this chapter, you will learn about the system that controls everything in your body—your nervous system. You will discover how this system receives and sends messages throughout your body, allowing you to react to the world around you.

The Parts of Your Nervous System

Your nervous system is made up of billions of specialized cells called **nerve cells.** The main job of a nerve cell is to receive messages and then send the messages to other cells. Nerve cells form bundles called **nerves.** Messages are received and sent from nerve cell to nerve cell along a nerve.

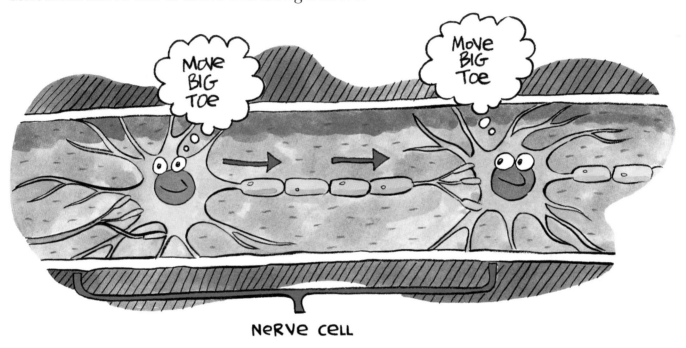

NERVE CELL

▲ Your nerve cells pass messages along a nerve.

Your **brain** is located inside your skull. It is made from nerve cells, as well. You can think of your brain as the control centre of your body. It receives messages from all parts of your body and sends out messages in return. Your brain is the main organ in your nervous system, but it cannot work alone. It needs help to receive and send messages. It gets this help from your nerves and spinal cord.

⇨ Learning Tip

Check for understanding as you read. After you read about each vocabulary word in this section, explain the meaning of each word to a partner.

Look at the words in brackets. How do they relate to sense organs? Explain to a partner what the brackets mean.

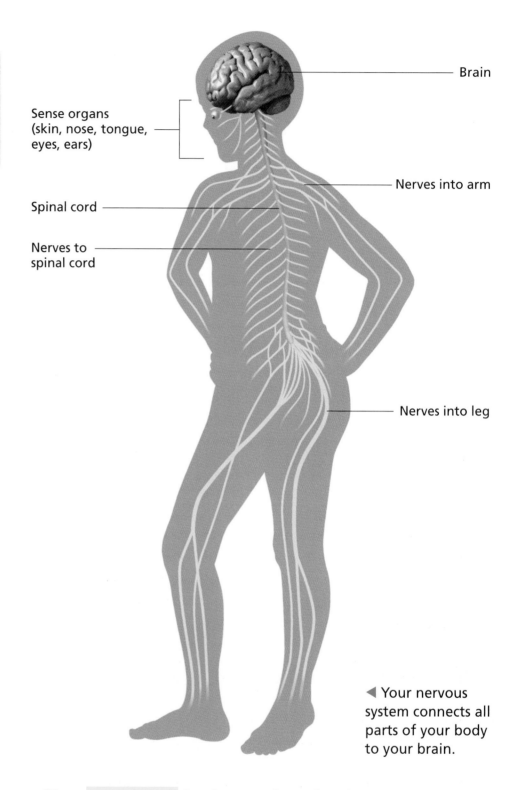

Brain

Sense organs (skin, nose, tongue, eyes, ears)

Nerves into arm

Spinal cord

Nerves to spinal cord

Nerves into leg

◄ Your nervous system connects all parts of your body to your brain.

Your **spinal cord** is a long rod, made of many nerves. It is located inside your spinal column. Your spinal column protects your spinal cord. Your spinal cord is attached to the base of your brain. It ends just before the bottom of your spinal column.

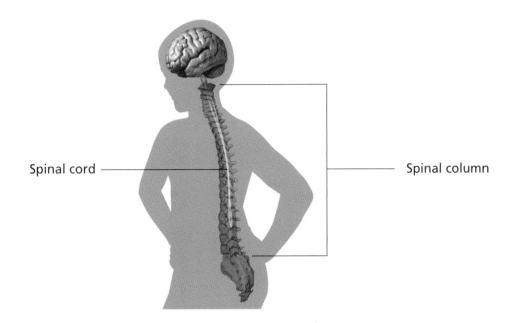

Spinal cord

Spinal column

◄ Your spinal cord helps carry messages to and from the brain. It is protected by the spinal column.

Look at the diagram of the nervous system on the previous page. There are 31 pairs of nerves that branch off the spinal cord. These nerves connect your brain with the rest of your body. They run to your head, feet, hands, and other parts of your body. As these nerves spread out, they branch many times. This allows nerves to reach every part of your body—even the smallest parts.

Your sense organs are also part of your nervous system. Your **sense organs** gather information from outside your body and send the information to your brain through nerves. Your sense organs include your skin, nose, tongue, eyes, and ears.

⇨ Check Your Understanding

1. Name the four main parts of your nervous system.
2. Why is the brain the most important organ of your nervous system?
3. Name your sense organs. What is their role in your nervous system?

2 The Brain: Your Control Centre

Your brain contains about 100 billion nerve cells. It is shaped like two clenched fists. It has a wrinkled appearance because its surface has many folds. This photo, taken from above, clearly shows these folds.

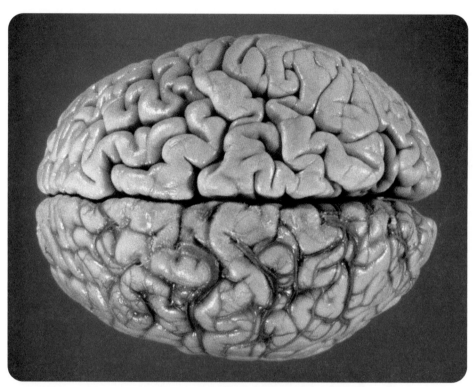

▲ Your brain is the control centre of your whole body.

Your brain controls everything you do. Messages are sent to your brain from every part of your body. Your brain takes in all the information and decides what to do. Then your brain sends a message back to the part of your body that needs to react.

If you bite an apple, your brain will tell your mouth to start digesting it. If you lose your balance, your brain will tell your muscles and bones to move quickly to regain your balance. Your brain controls how you react to everything around you and inside you.

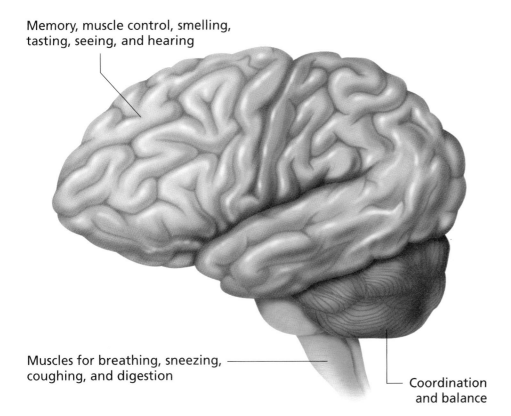

Memory, muscle control, smelling, tasting, seeing, and hearing

Muscles for breathing, sneezing, coughing, and digestion

Coordination and balance

◀ Each of your brain's three parts has its own important jobs.

Your brain has three main parts. Look at the diagram above. The part that is coloured grey is the largest part. It is the part that receives messages from your sense organs. It is the thinking and reasoning part of your brain, so it takes the messages, thinks about them, and decides what to do. Your memories are stored here. As well, this part of your brain tells your muscles what to do.

The part of the brain that is red in the diagram keeps you coordinated and balanced. It coordinates the movements of your muscles, so they operate smoothly when you are walking and running. It tells your body which arms and legs to move. It helps your body keep its balance so that you do not fall over.

The part of the brain that is green in the diagram sits at the base of the brain, at the top of the spinal cord. This is the part of the brain that controls muscles for things like heart rate, breathing, digestion, coughing, and sneezing. You don't think about these things happening. They just happen because this part of your brain is always working and keeping them going.

⊙ **Learning Tip**

The diagram above uses colour to show the main parts of the brain. After you read about each part, find the colour on the diagram and read the label that goes with it.

The diagram below shows what might happen in your body when you see and pick up a glass of milk. What part of your brain do you use to do this?

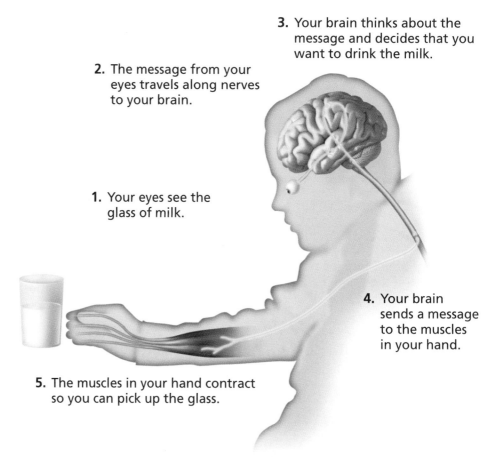

3. Your brain thinks about the message and decides that you want to drink the milk.

2. The message from your eyes travels along nerves to your brain.

1. Your eyes see the glass of milk.

4. Your brain sends a message to the muscles in your hand.

5. The muscles in your hand contract so you can pick up the glass.

▲ A long chain of messages runs through your nervous system from the moment you look at a glass of milk to the moment you pick it up to drink.

Reflex Actions

Not all messages and reactions to messages travel through your brain. Have you ever moved your hand away suddenly from a hot object, or jumped at the sound of a loud, unexpected noise? If so, you have experienced a reflex. A **reflex** is a response that occurs immediately and automatically. Because you need to respond so quickly, the message does not go to your brain. It only goes to your spinal cord. Nerve cells in your spinal cord send a message back to your body, telling your body how to react.

Try This

Observe a Reflex

Skills Focus: observing, interpreting data

 Do not tap your partner's leg too hard. Be careful when sitting on the desk.

1. Do this activity with a partner. Have your partner sit on a desk. The desk must be high enough that your partner's toes do not touch the floor.

2. With the edge of your hand (the little finger side), give your partner's leg a quick, light tap, just below the kneecap.

3. Switch places with your partner, and repeat steps 1 and 2.

4. What happened to your partner when you tapped his or her leg? Explain why this is an example of a reflex.

⇨ Check Your Understanding

1. Why is your brain so important? What role does it play in your body?

2. If someone is paralyzed from the waist down, what can you infer about her or his spinal cord?

3. How would your body react if you accidentally touched something very hot or very cold?

③ *Conduct an Investigation*

SKILLS MENU

- ○ Questioning
- ● Measuring
- ● Predicting
- ○ Classifying
- ○ Designing Experiments
- ○ Inferring
- ● Interpreting Data
- ● Fair Testing
- ● Observing
- ● Communicating

Test Your Reaction Time

Your reaction time is the length of time it takes for a message to travel to your brain, and then from your brain to the muscles in your body to make them move. Sometimes you can improve your reaction time. In this investigation, you will work with a partner to see how quickly you can catch a ruler and find out if you can improve your reaction time.

Question

Can I improve my reaction time with practice?

Prediction

Make a prediction about whether your reaction time can be improved with practice.

Materials

- 30 cm ruler

ruler

Procedure

Step 1 Copy the following table into your notebook.

Data Table for Investigation 7.3		
Trial	Where ruler caught (cm)	Reaction time (seconds)
1		
2		
3		
4		
5		

Step 2 Have your partner stand with his or her writing arm held straight out, and with the thumb and fingers about 2 cm apart.

Step 3 Hold a 30 cm ruler above your partner's hand, with the 0 mark at the bottom. The end of the ruler should be between your partner's thumb and index finger. Your partner's thumb and index finger should not touch the ruler.

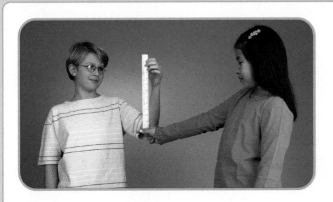

Step 6 Repeat steps 2 to 5 four times.

Step 7 Change roles with your partner, and repeat steps 2 to 6.

Step 8 Complete the third column of your table, using the table below.

Step 4 Drop the ruler without warning your partner. Your partner will catch the ruler by closing his or her thumb and fingers.

Step 5 Read the ruler to find out how far it dropped before your partner caught it. Read the number that is just above your partner's thumb and index finger. Your partner will record the distance in his or her table.

Find Your Reaction Time

Where ruler caught (cm)	Reaction time (seconds)
5	0.10
10	0.14
15	0.17
20	0.20
25	0.23
30	0.25

Interpret Data and Observations

1. What happened to your reaction time between trials?

2. Was your prediction correct?

3. What do you think would happen if you tried to catch the ruler 10 times in a row?

Apply and Extend

1. How would being tired affect your reaction time? Design a simple experiment to test this.

⇨ Check Your Understanding

1. Was this a fair test? Give reasons to support your answer.

4 Your Senses

Like all humans, you have special sense organs—your skin, nose, tongue, eyes, and ears. The nerves in your sense organs send messages to your brain. Your brain recognizes these messages as sensations—touch, smell, taste, sight, and sound.

⇨ Learning Tip

Each of the next five paragraphs tells you about one of the sense organs. After you finish reading each paragraph, tell a partner what you have learned about each organ.

If you touch your skin, you can feel your hand on your skin. If you put something hot or cold on your skin, you can feel the warmth or coolness on your skin. You can feel these sensations because your skin has very small nerves that pick up these sensations and send the messages to your brain.

Inside your nose are nerves that react to smell. When you smell something, the nerves in your nose take in the smell and send the message to your brain.

There are taste buds on your tongue. Taste buds are nerves that react to different taste sensations. Taste buds take in the taste and send the message to your brain.

Your eyes have nerves that take in images, or pictures. They send the pictures to your brain so that you can see what is in your world.

Your ears have nerves that pick up sound vibrations. The nerves in your ears sense these vibrations and send them as messages to your brain.

In all these cases, your brain uses its reasoning and memory to think about and figure out what it is feeling, smelling, tasting, seeing, or hearing.

 Compare Your Sense of Touch

Skills Focus: observing, interpreting data, communicating

 Do not keep the ice on any place for longer than 15 seconds.

1. Work with a partner. Your teacher will give you two sealed plastic bags. Each bag will have a piece of ice in it.

2. Close your eyes. Have your partner place one bag on the inside of one of your wrists and the other bag on the outside of the same wrist. Which part of your wrist feels colder? Record your observations in a data table.

3. Have your partner place one bag on top of one of your hands and the other bag on the palm of the same hand. Which part of your hand feels colder? Record your observations in a data table.

4. Switch roles with your partner, and repeat steps 2 and 3.

5. Compare your observations with your partner's observations.

6. What did you learn about your sense of touch from this activity?

⇨ Check Your Understanding

1. How are all your sense organs the same?
2. What is the relationship between your brain and your sense organs?

How Your Nervous System Interacts with Other Systems

You have learned that your nervous system is connected to every part of your body. This means that it is connected to all the other systems in your body. The organs in your other systems send messages to your brain. Your brain sends messages back, telling the organs what to do.

Imagine that you are sitting, doing your homework. Suddenly, you feel something on your arm. It's a mosquito, and it has just bitten you. What happens in your body?

Scratching a mosquito bite may seem like a simple thing to do, but three systems are involved—your nervous, muscular, and skeletal systems.

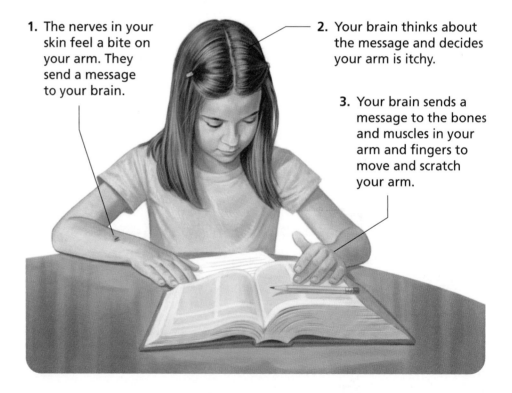

1. The nerves in your skin feel a bite on your arm. They send a message to your brain.

2. Your brain thinks about the message and decides your arm is itchy.

3. Your brain sends a message to the bones and muscles in your arm and fingers to move and scratch your arm.

Here is another example of how your nervous system interacts with the other systems in your body. Suppose you are hungry when you come home from school. You see a banana and an apple on the kitchen counter. What happens in your body?

1. Your eyes see the banana and the apple, and the nerves in your eyes send this message to your brain.

2. Your brain thinks about the message. It decides that you are hungry and want the banana because you have already had an apple today.

3. Your brain sends the message to the muscles and bones in your arm to reach for the banana, peel it, and take a bite.

4. Your brain sends a message to the muscles in your jaw to start chewing the piece of banana.

5. Your brain sends another message to your esophagus to swallow the piece of banana and move it down to your stomach.

6. Your brain sends a message to your stomach to start digesting.

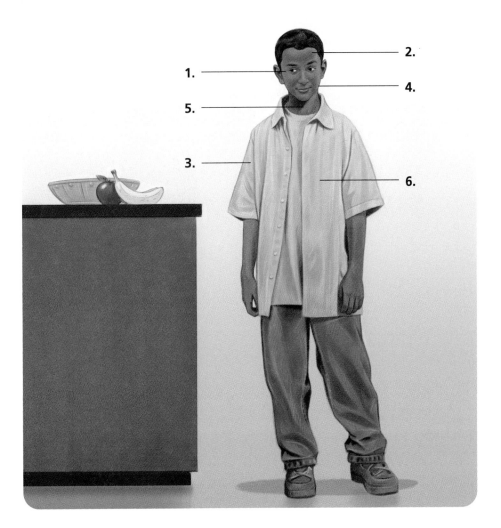

How many body systems were involved in this simple act of peeling a banana and swallowing a piece of it?

In both of these examples, your sense organs took in sensations and sent messages to your brain. Your brain responded and sent messages back to specific parts of your body. What your body does every waking and sleeping minute of your life depends completely on your powerful nervous system and the way it works with your other body systems.

⇨ Check Your Understanding

1. Suppose that you are playing soccer and see a ball coming toward you. What will happen in your body? Describe two possible responses, and the body systems that are involved.

Chapter Review

Your nervous system controls all your other body systems.

Key Idea: Your brain is the control centre of your body.

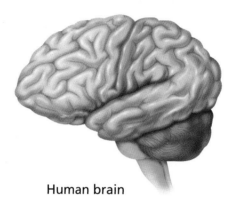

Human brain

Vocabulary

brain p. 139

Key Idea: Nerves send messages to and from your brain to all parts of your body.

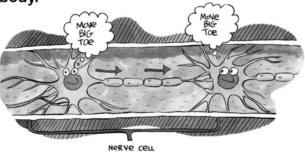

Vocabulary

nerve cells p. 139
nerves p. 139
spinal cord p. 140
reflex p. 144

Key Idea: Your sense organs react to touch, smell, taste, sight, and sound.

Vocabulary

sense organs
  p. 141

Key Idea: Your nervous system is connected to all the other systems in your body.

1. The nerves in your skin feel a bite on your arm. They send a message to your brain.

2. Your brain thinks about the message and decides your arm is itchy.

3. Your brain sends a message to the bones and muscles in your arm and fingers to move and scratch your arm.

Review Key Ideas and Vocabulary

Use the vocabulary words in your answers to the questions.

1. Copy the following table into your notebook. List each part of the nervous system and its main job.

Part of nervous system	Job

2. Make a web about the three main parts of the brain and what each part does.

3. Why are reflexes important?

4. If there were no nerves running from your feet to your brain, what would happen if you stubbed your toe on a rock?

Visit the Quiz Centre at: www·science·nelson·com GO

Apply What You've Learned

Role-Play Your Nervous System

Looking Back

You have learned

- how nerves send messages from all parts of your body to your brain, and from your brain back to your body
- how your sense organs react to touch, smell, taste, sight, and sound
- that your nervous system is connected to all the other systems in your body

In this activity, you will work in a group and use what you have learned about the nervous system to role-play what happens in your body when you react to a sensation.

Demonstrate Your Learning

Develop a Role-Play

1. Brainstorm a list of simple sensations that you have experienced. Here are some examples:
   - seeing a light turn red just before you cross a street and stopping
   - smelling freshly baked cookies and eating one
   - stepping on hot sand in your bare feet and then running off the sand

2. Choose a sensation from your list to role-play. Then identify
   - the messages that need to be sent to the brain or automatically to different parts of the body (Remember that some messages may only go to the spinal cord.)
   - the parts of the nervous system that will carry the messages
   - the parts of the body that will receive and send the messages
   - the ways that different parts of the body will react to the messages

3. Plan your role-play. Decide on how your group will
   - communicate the messages to the audience (Will you speak the messages, write the messages on cards, or use a combination of both?)
   - show the messages being passed from one body part to another
   - show the reactions of the body parts

Perform a Role-Play
1. Practise your role-play, and then perform it for your class. Be prepared to explain what each player is doing and why.

> ⇨ **Assessment Checklist**

DEVELOPING THE ROLE-PLAY
As you develop each role in your role-play, make sure that you show you are able to

✔ identify correctly the role of each part of the nervous system
✔ show how each part of the nervous system works
✔ show how different parts of the body react to messages from the nervous system
✔ use science words correctly

PERFORMING THE ROLE-PLAY
As you put on your role-play, make sure that you show you are able to

✔ work cooperatively with your group

Making Connections

Create a Road Map of Your Body

Looking Back

In this unit, you have learned
- how your digestive system processes food to make nutrients for your cells
- how your respiratory system takes in oxygen for your cells
- how your circulatory system transports nutrients and oxygen throughout your body
- how your excretory system gets rid of wastes from your cells
- how your muscular and skeletal systems allow you to move and, with your skin, support and protect your other body systems
- how your nervous system controls other body systems

In this activity, you will use your understanding of these major body systems to create a road map of your body.

Demonstrate Your Learning

Plan a Road Map
1. Use the four chapters in this unit to identify the information about each body system that you want to include on your map.

2. Examine real maps to find ideas that you can use to show different things on your map. Decide how you will show points of interest (organs) and the roads (veins, arteries, and nerves) that connect these points of interest. Choose colours and symbols for each body system so that your map is easy to read and follow.

3. Decide on the order in which you will add the information about each body system to your map.

Create a Road Map

1. Draw your map in pencil. Look for places where the information is too crowded. Add shapes, symbols, labels, and any other information. Make a key or legend to explain what the different colours, shapes, and symbols mean.

2. Explain your map to at least one classmate. Ask for feedback, and make changes based on the feedback. Then colour your map.

3. Post your completed map for others in your class to read.

⇨ Assessment Checklist

PLANNING THE ROAD MAP
Your plan should show that you are able to

- ✔ identify important information about the body systems you have studied in this unit to include on your map
- ✔ create a design that will present the information in a readable form on paper

CREATING THE ROAD MAP
Your road map should show that you are able to

- ✔ accurately show the body systems you have studied in this unit and the ways they are connected
- ✔ use colour, shapes, symbols, and other features such as legends to help readers follow your map
- ✔ use science words correctly

Unit C

Earth's Resources

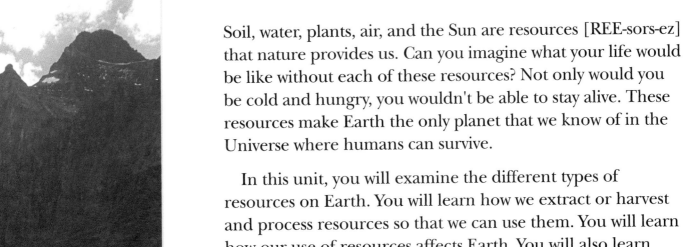

Preview

Soil, water, plants, air, and the Sun are resources [REE-sors-ez] that nature provides us. Can you imagine what your life would be like without each of these resources? Not only would you be cold and hungry, you wouldn't be able to stay alive. These resources make Earth the only planet that we know of in the Universe where humans can survive.

In this unit, you will examine the different types of resources on Earth. You will learn how we extract or harvest and process resources so that we can use them. You will learn how our use of resources affects Earth. You will also learn how traditional Aboriginal cultures in British Columbia use resources responsibly. You will also explore ways we can all protect Earth's resources for future generations.

 Try This

Brainstorm Resources

Skills Focus: communicating

1. With a partner, brainstorm a list of resources that are found on Earth.

2. Now circle all the resources that you think are found in British Columbia.

3. Compare your list with the list of another pair of students. Add to your list any other resources that you think are found in British Columbia.

4. Add to your list as you work through this unit.

◄ Resources like soil, water, plants, air, and the Sun make it possible for humans to survive on Earth.

We depend on Earth's natural resources for our survival.

Key Ideas

▸ Everything we use comes from Earth.

▸ Resources can be living or non-living.

▸ The way we use resources has an impact on the environment.

▸ We can help to conserve resources by using them wisely.

Think of the things you used today before you left your home. Where did the materials in your toothbrush come from? Where did the water in your bathroom tap come from? Where did the electricity to run the lights in your home come from?

No matter what things you think about, they are products of Earth. Earth provides us with every single thing we use in our daily lives.

In this chapter, you will learn about Earth's resources and how humans use Earth's resources to survive. You will also learn how our use of resources affects our environment, and how we can use resources more wisely.

Earth's Natural Resources

▲ Our environment is made of living and non-living things.

Have you ever observed the things around you when you were outside? You may have noticed that some things, such as plants and animals, are living. All living things can grow, move, and use energy. Other things, such as rocks and clouds, are not living. They do not grow, move on their own, or use energy. All living and non-living things are part of Earth's environment.

Together, the living and non-living things in Earth's environment give us everything we need to survive. They also give us everything we want to make our lives more comfortable or enjoyable.

All the things we use to meet our needs and wants come from Earth's natural resources. **Natural resources** are all the living and non-living materials in nature. Natural resources can be living plants and animals, or non-living materials, such as water, wind, and gold. We call these materials **resources** because we can use them to meet our wants and needs.

Classify British Columbia's Living and Non-Living Resources

Skills Focus: classifying, inferring, communicating

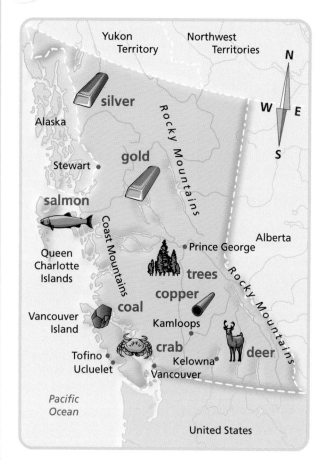

1. Copy the following T-chart into your notebook.

Living resources	Non-living resources

2. Look at the map of natural resources found in British Columbia. Think about whether each resource is living or non-living. Record each resource in the correct column of your T-chart.

3. Add two living resources and two non-living resources that are not on the map but are also found in British Columbia.

4. Share your T-chart with your classmates.

Resources We Use

Early peoples hunted animals and searched for food that grew naturally, such as berries. They made their homes in caves or built their homes out of wood from trees. Think about the resources you use today. Some are the same resources that people used in the past, and they may be used for the same purposes. For example, you use water for many of the same purposes, such as drinking and washing. Your bed, bookshelves, and other furniture may be made of wood. You may eat fish or other seafood. It is easy to identify the resources used in these three examples.

However, it is not so easy to identify other resources we use today. New technologies can change a resource so that it can be used in different ways. One example is petroleum [puh-TRO-lee-uhm], or what we call oil. Petroleum is a resource found beneath Earth's surface. It can be used to make gasoline for cars and buses. It can also be used to make polyester (a fabric used in clothing), as well as plastics, paints, fertilizers, and many other products. None of these products look like petroleum does when it comes from the ground.

⟡ **Learning Tip**

The word "petroleum" comes from *petra-*, which means "rock" and *-oleum*, which means "oil." So, petroleum simply means "oil from rock."

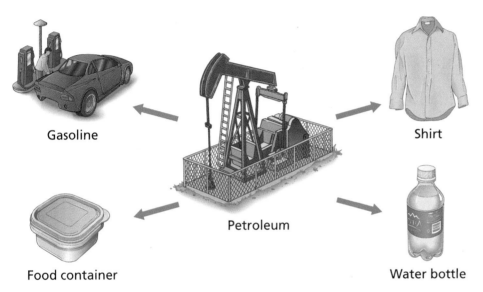

Gasoline

Shirt

Petroleum

Food container

Water bottle

▲ The same resource can be used to run a car and to make plastic products and some parts of clothes.

Today, we use resources to make products that were unknown to people in the past—from MP3 players to artificial limbs. No matter how a product is made or what it looks like, it comes from Earth's resources.

⟡ Check Your Understanding

1. Where does everything we use come from?
2. Think about the student book you are reading. Can you identify the resources used to make it? Why is it sometimes difficult to identify the natural resources that are used to make something?

2 The Impact of Resource Use

Clean Up an Oil Spill

Skills Focus: predicting, observing, communicating

1. Measure 15 mL of olive oil. Add the oil to 250 mL of water in a bowl. Mix the oil into the water as much as possible.
2. Make a table like the one below.

	Oil removal method	Observations	Questions

3. Use whatever you think will work best to remove the oil. For example, you could try mopping it up with a paper towel or sponge. Record what you did, what you observed, and any questions you have.
4. Were you able to remove all the oil from the water?
5. Share your findings in a group. Based on what you learned, what techniques would you suggest for cleaning up oil spills in lakes or oceans?

As you discovered in the activity, it is hard to remove all the oil from water. It is hard to undo damage. Things that can change the environment are said to have an **environmental impact** [en-VI-ruhn-MEN-tl IHM-pakt]. Environmental impacts can be small or large.

▶ Oil spills have an environmental impact on the water and everything that lives in the water.

How Ecosystems Work

All living things interact with each other and with the non-living things in their environment. The system that is formed by the interactions of all the living and non-living things in an environment is called an **ecosystem** [EE-ko-sis-tuhm]. Ecosystems can be small, like a puddle or a tree. They can also be large, like a forest, a lake, or an entire valley.

⟲ **Learning Tip**

What does the word "interactions" mean? Read this paragraph again to help you define it. Then check your definition in a dictionary.

▲ What living and non-living things can you see in this ecosystem?

All the living and non-living things in an ecosystem are connected. This means that a change in one part of the ecosystem can affect the whole ecosystem. A terrarium [tuh-RARE-ee-uhm] is an artificial ecosystem. The water, air, light, temperature, plants, animals, and soil in a terrarium all work together. When the plants in a terrarium have the right light, water, temperature, and nutrients in the soil, they are able to live. When the plants have what they need to live, the animals that live off the plants, such as butterflies, are able to live.

Ecosystems in nature work the same way as an ecosystem in a terrarium.

▲ In a terrarium, a single change can affect all the other parts of the ecosystem. This is also true in a natural ecosystem.

The natural resources we use are parts of ecosystems. When we use one of these resources, we are making an environmental impact on an ecosystem because we are changing the ecosystem. Humans often benefit from the changes to an ecosystem, but the environmental impact is always there.

Traditional Aboriginal Cultures and Resources

Aboriginal peoples have lived in what is now known as British Columbia for thousands of years. In traditional Aboriginal communities, the people understand how they and all the living and non-living things in their environment are connected. They understand that if one part of an ecosystem is affected, everything else in the ecosystem is also affected. They try to take from Earth only what they need to survive. They also try to waste as little as possible of what they take from Earth. For example, in the traditional culture of the Kutenai [KOOT-nee] people, if an elk is killed for food, its hide is used to make clothing and its bones and antlers are used to make tools.

◄ Aboriginal peoples use the circle to represent harmony and connections in nature. Everything in the circle is important and equal. Humans are part of the circle, so they are only one of the many important parts of nature.

If we want to continue to enjoy Earth's resources, we must understand how the living and non-living things on Earth are connected and how we are connected to them. If we learn to use resources responsibly, we can protect them so they will still be available in the future.

⇨ Check Your Understanding

1. What is an ecosystem? Describe how Earth is a large ecosystem.
2. Traditional Aboriginal cultures eat berries, fish, shellfish, and many other plants and animals that are found in their local environments. How do you think these cultures protect the ecosystems in which these plants and animals live?

3 Conserving Resources

Learning Tip

Before you read this section, make a web to show what you already know about conserving resources.

We use resources every day. Sometimes we don't think about where a resource came from or how hard it would be to replace if it was all used up. Our actions can have serious effects on the resource, and on the environment.

Conservation means saving or reusing resources so they will be available for the future. The governments of Canada and British Columbia have passed many laws and regulations to help conserve our resources and protect the environment. For example, there are laws about when people can fish, where they can fish, what fish they can catch, and how many fish they can catch.

▲ Dungeness crabs, like the ones above, are caught in traps. People who catch crabs must have a licence and can only fish in certain areas. They can only use a specific number of traps, and the crabs they catch must be a certain size.

It is not only governments and companies that can help to conserve our resources. You can help, too!

How You Can Help

Classify Your Garbage

Skills Focus: classifying, communicating

1. Make a table with the following headings.

	Paper	Plastic	Glass	Metal	Food waste

2. For one day, record everything you throw away as garbage in the correct column of your table. Make sure that you include *everything*.

3. At the end of the day, add up the garbage items in each column. Then rank the columns from the least number of items (5) to the most number of items (1).

4. Compare your table with some of your classmates' tables. Discuss what you could change to create less garbage.

We all need to think about the resources we use and how to conserve them.

Reduce

The best way to conserve resources is to reduce what we use. By reducing, we use fewer resources and create less garbage. The less garbage we create, the less garbage there is to manage. You can reduce by doing simple things such as using both sides of a piece of paper for writing or turning off lights when you're not in a room. You can also reduce by paying attention to the packaging on the things you buy. The less packaging there is, the less garbage you create.

▲ Can you think of another way to buy raisins that uses less packaging?

Reuse

Another way to save resources is to reuse them. Reusing means using a product again, or using it for a different purpose, before throwing it away or recycling it. When you reuse, you don't have to buy so many new products. Garage sales and stores that sell used clothing give people the chance to buy and reuse clothing and other items that might end up in landfills. Wrapping paper and gift bags can be reused many times. Shoeboxes can be used to store things.

Recycle

A third way to save resources is to buy products in containers that can be recycled. **Recycling** means that a container can be processed and then used again. One example is aluminum cans. Aluminum cans can be sent to a factory to be made into aluminum sheets, which can be made into new aluminum cans. This way, the same aluminum is used over and over again. Recycling aluminum cans helps to save aluminum so that less needs to be mined. Glass, plastic, and paper products (such as newspapers, cardboard containers, and writing paper) can also be recycled to make new products.

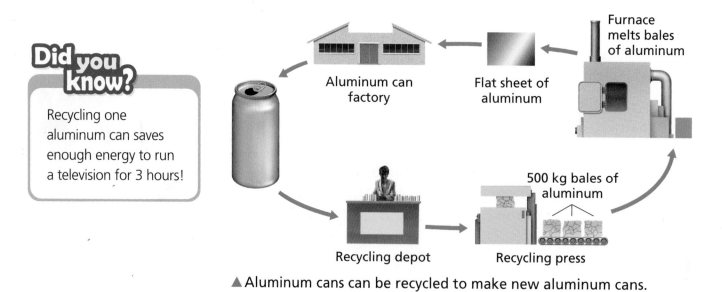

Aluminum can factory

Flat sheet of aluminum

Furnace melts bales of aluminum

Recycling depot

Recycling press

500 kg bales of aluminum

▲ Aluminum cans can be recycled to make new aluminum cans.

Composting

Another form of recycling is called composting. In composting, bacteria and other small organisms, such as worms, break down matter. Matter is material that was once living, such as vegetable and fruit scraps. Composting makes a material called compost. Compost can be used as a fertilizer to make better soil.

▲ Composting is a good way to recycle kitchen waste to make compost. The compost that is created can go back into the soil to help grow new plants.

Products that are made from materials that were once living are **biodegradable** [BY-oh-dih-GRAY-duh-buhl]. This means that they can be broken down by organisms, just like fruit and vegetable scraps can. For example, paper is a biodegradable product because it is made from trees that were once living.

⇨ Check Your Understanding

1. What is conservation? Give an example to explain why conservation is important.
2. List three different ways to conserve resources, and give an example of each.
3. Name one product that is biodegradable and one product that is not biodegradable. Explain the difference between these products.

Chapter Review

We depend on Earth's natural resources for our survival.

Key Idea: **Everything we use comes from Earth.**

Vocabulary
natural resources
  p. 161
resources p. 161

Key Idea: **Resources can be living or non-living.**

Key Idea: **The way we use resources has an impact on the environment.**

Vocabulary
**environmental
  impact** p. 164
ecosystem p. 165

Key Idea: We can help to conserve resources by using them wisely.

Vocabulary

conservation p. 168

recycling p. 170

biodegradable
  p. 171

Review Key Ideas and Vocabulary

Use the vocabulary words in your answers to the questions.

1. Where do we get natural resources?

2. Identify the living and non-living resources in this picture.

3. Use an example to describe how our use of resources can have an impact on the environment.

4. What can we do to help conserve resources?

Apply What You've Learned

Design a School Conservation Plan

Looking Back

You have learned

- that everything we use comes from Earth's resources
- that how we use resources has an impact on the environment
- that there are many ways to conserve resources

In this activity, you will work with a group to design a simple conservation plan for your school. Your conservation plan must be easy to put into practice, with little or no cost.

Demonstrate Your Learning

Do Research for Your Plan

1. Take a look around your school to find out how your school is recycling, reusing, and reducing. For example, is waste paper put in garbage cans or in recycling boxes? Look in both classrooms and common areas, such as hallways and the gymnasium.

2. Choose two or three members of your group to interview teachers, the principal, and support staff to find out what they do to conserve resources in your school. Have other group members interview students to find out what they do to conserve resources in school.

3. Create a list of things that are now being done to conserve resources in your school.

Develop and Present Your Plan

1. Make a list of new things that could be done to conserve resources. Make sure that your ideas are simple and would cost nothing or very little to do.

2. Think of how you might convince people in your school to do these new things.

3. Choose three ideas from your list for your conservation plan. Decide on the best way to communicate your ideas.

> ⇨ **Assessment Checklist**
>
> CONSERVATION PLAN
>
> **As you conduct research, and develop and present your plan, make sure that you show you are able to**
>
> ✔ identify ways that your school is conserving resources
> ✔ create a conservation plan that is simple and would cost nothing or very little to do
> ✔ communicate your ideas clearly

Renewable resources can replace themselves.

▶ We harvest and process renewable resources to meet our needs.

▶ Harvesting and processing renewable resources has an impact on the environment.

▶ Traditional Aboriginal cultures protect and conserve resources.

▶ We must conserve and protect our renewable resources for future use.

For thousands of years, Aboriginal peoples have used the natural resources around them to survive. They have managed the living and non-living things in their environment so that the resources they depend on return each year. All British Columbians depend on the same resources, but we use them for many different and new purposes. We also use more of them.

In this chapter, you will study three renewable resources that are very important to British Columbians: salmon [SAH-muhn], forests, and water. You will learn how these resources are harvested and processed to meet many of our needs. You will also learn how traditional Aboriginal cultures conserve these resources. Finally, you will learn what all British Columbians must do to make sure that our renewable resources are available to meet our future needs.

Renewable Resources

Forests are an important natural resource in British Columbia. We use trees to make many products, such as furniture, paper, and cardboard. How can we cut down so many trees to make wood products and still have so many trees left? Some of Earth's resources can replace themselves through reproduction, be re-grown, or renew themselves naturally. These resources are called **renewable** [rih-NOO-uh-buhl] resources. They will always be available if we use them carefully.

Living Renewable Resources

▲ Many renewable resources are living things, such as trees, fish, and animals in the wild.

Living resources are part of the cycle of life and death. A living resource produces more of its kind while it lives, and then it dies. Plants grow from seeds, and fish reproduce by laying eggs.

Non-Living Renewable Resources

Non-living resources can also be renewable. We consider these resources to be renewable because they are almost always there for us to use. Non-living renewable resources include water, wind, air, and the Sun.

▲ Non-living renewable resources are important to living things. Water is the home for fish, other animals, and water plants. Plants need the Sun to grow. Wind provides the power to move people in boats.

British Columbia's Renewable Resources

Renewable resources are found everywhere in British Columbia. There are fish and other animals in streams, rivers, and the Pacific Ocean. There are trees in the coastal rain forests and inland mountains. There are resources that provide energy, such as water, wind, and the Sun, nearly everywhere. The map on the next page shows just a few of British Columbia's renewable resources.

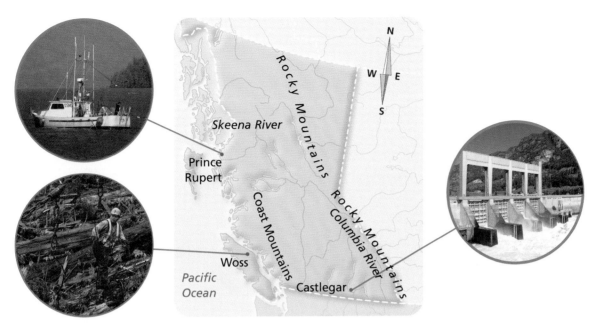

▲ A map showing some of British Columbia's renewable resources.

 Try This

Identify Renewable Resources

Skills Focus: classifying, communicating

1. List three renewable resources in your community.

2. Write one or two sentences to explain why each resource is renewable. For example, suppose that one of the resources you listed is trees. You could explain that trees are renewable because they make seeds, which grow into new trees.

3. Compare ideas in a group. Do you all agree that the resources you listed are renewable? Do you all agree on why they are renewable?

➡ Check Your Understanding

1. What makes a resource renewable?

2. List five different renewable resources. Give an example of each resource, and describe how humans use it.

3. Why are water, wind, air, and the Sun considered to be renewable resources, even though they are non-living?

2 Salmon

▲ Sockeye salmon like these are one of British Columbia's valuable renewable resources.

Salmon are an important natural resource in British Columbia. They are a valuable resource in commercial fishing, sport fishing, aquaculture (fish farming), and processing.

Harvesting Salmon

Harvesting is taking any resource, including water, from Earth's surface. This means that fish, such as salmon, are harvested, even though we usually use the words "fished" and "caught" instead of "harvested." Many different methods of salmon harvesting have been used in British Columbia.

Salmon are highly valued by the Aboriginal peoples of British Columbia. For thousands of years, they have been harvested by Aboriginal peoples using traditional methods. These methods do not catch a lot of salmon at a time, and they allow the number and kind of salmon caught to be controlled. Today, most salmon that are harvested using traditional methods are used for personal food and ceremonies.

⇨ Learning Tip

Check your understanding as you read this section. Pause after each paragraph and try to explain what you have just read, using your own words.

Harvesting fish to sell is called commercial fishing. Commercial fishers need to catch large numbers of salmon. To do this, they use different methods than traditional fishers. It is difficult to control how many salmon are caught using commercial fishing methods. As well, these methods often catch other fish and marine life along with the salmon.

Salmon can also be farmed. This is called aquaculture. In fish farms, the salmon are raised in closed pens, mostly in the ocean. They are fed special feed pellets. When they are large enough, they are harvested and sold. About three quarters of the salmon raised on fish farms in British Columbia are Atlantic salmon. This kind of salmon is not naturally found in the Pacific Ocean.

▲ Catching salmon using a weir [WEER].

▲ Catching salmon using a seine [SAYN] net. The seine net is attached to the boat.

▲ Some salmon are raised in fish farms, like this one in the Burdwood Islands.

Many salmon are caught in sport fishing, as well. Another name for sport fishing is recreational fishing. Recreational fishing is an important part of British Columbia's tourist industry. Many people from other parts of Canada and the world come to British Columbia to fish and to enjoy the natural beauty of the province.

Processing Salmon

People do not use most living resources exactly as they are harvested. Usually, the resources are processed. When a resource is processed, it is changed from its natural form into another form. Salmon are processed so they will taste different or to preserve them (make them last longer).

In the past, Aboriginal peoples processed the salmon they caught so they could eat salmon year-round. The salmon were air-dried or smoked on cedar sticks around a fire. Drying or smoking the salmon removed the moisture from them, so they would not rot. Today, these traditional methods continue to be used in Aboriginal communities.

▲ Aboriginal peoples continue to smoke salmon today using traditional methods.

Starting in the early 1800s, European settlers used salt to preserve salmon. The salmon were salted and transported back to Europe in barrels. By 1867, canneries were operating in British Columbia. In canning, the salmon are cleaned and packed into metal cans with lids. The cans are then heated to remove the air and cook the salmon. Canning is still an important process for preserving commercially harvested salmon. As well, many salmon are frozen, smoked, and sold fresh.

Protecting the Salmon Industry

The number of salmon in British Columbia's waters today is much lower than it was in the past. There are many opinions about why the number of salmon is decreasing. Some of these opinions are

- increased fishing
- an increase in the temperature of Pacific Ocean water
- the destruction of streams and rivers where salmon lay eggs
- the infection of wild salmon with lice from farmed salmon

How can we save the salmon? Governments have passed laws about the kind of salmon and the number that can be caught each year. Groups of people are protecting and restoring environments where salmon lay their eggs. Governments, scientists, Aboriginal peoples, environmentalists, fishers, fish farmers, and other interested people are working together to find ways to protect our salmon for the future.

⇨ Learning Tip

Think about what you have read. How do you think British Columbia's salmon should be protected? Compare your opinion with a partner's opinion.

⇨ Check Your Understanding

1. Use a Venn diagram to compare the similarities and differences between traditional Aboriginal methods for harvesting salmon and commercial fishing.

2. Why do you think salmon farming started?

3. Create a flow chart to show what happens to a salmon from the time it is caught until a sandwich is made from a tin of salmon.

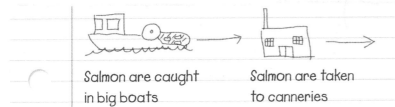

Salmon are caught in big boats   Salmon are taken to canneries

4. Why does the salmon industry need to be protected? How is this being done?

③ *Forests*

▶ A black spruce forest in Northern British Columbia.

Trees have always been one of the most important natural resources in British Columbia. In the past, the Aboriginal peoples of British Columbia used trees for shelter, transportation, cooking, storage, clothing, and medicine.

Today, we still value trees for the products they can give us. Logging and making forestry products are important industries in British Columbia. Many people earn a living in tourism because thousands of people visit our forests each year. As well, our forests help to keep our environment healthy by providing a habitat for many living things.

Logging Forests

Logging has become British Columbia's largest renewable resource industry. In the past, logging was done mainly by clear-cutting. Today, more companies are leaving some trees standing in areas that are logged. This is called selective logging. Tree seedlings that have been grown in plant nurseries are usually planted to replace the logged trees.

Roads are built to move people, equipment, and logs in and out of logging areas. Sometimes, in coastal forests, helicopters are used to lift trees out of logging areas. Using helicopters limits the amount of road building needed.

Did you know?

Aboriginal peoples in traditional communities still use the lodgepole pine for many purposes. They use the wood to build homes. They use the pine sap in medicines to treat muscle and joint pains and to relieve sore throats. In the spring, they strip and eat the sweet inner bark of the tree.

▲ In clear-cutting, all the trees in an area are cut down.

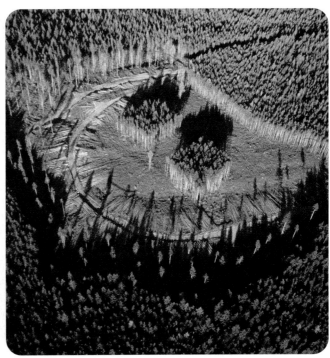

▲ In selective logging, some trees are cut down and others are left standing.

Managing forests is difficult. People who work in the forestry industry today try to use nature as a guide to find out the best way to log. They look at how trees are naturally removed and replaced in ecosystems in different areas. Then they use what they have learned to decide how many trees can be logged and what type of logging to use. They have learned that different kinds of logging are best for different ecosystems.

⇨ Learning Tip

Visuals can help you remember important information. What does each of these photos show? Is it helpful to have them side by side?

The Impact of Logging

When only a few trees are harvested at a time, the impact on the local environment is small. The **local environment** includes all the living and non-living things in a particular area.

As more trees are harvested, more of the local environment is affected. Bark, twigs, and mud can collect in the streams and rivers near logging sites. This can cause changes to the habitats of animals and plants that live in and along the rivers. Many places where salmon go to lay their eggs are destroyed.

When logging is not done carefully, soil may wash away. As a result, new plants cannot grow and animal habitats are changed. This can cause the populations of some animals to get smaller. Other animals may move to new habitats.

▶ The spotted owl and the mountain caribou are two animals that are endangered and could become extinct because their habitat of old forest is being logged.

⇨ **Learning Tip**

Check your understanding. Explain the impact of logging to a partner.

As logging increased, the government of British Columbia realized that laws were needed to make sure that forest ecosystems were protected. For example, there are now certain areas that cannot be logged and other areas that are logged less. Areas that are logged are replanted to speed up the growth of new trees. Many Aboriginal peoples are taking a greater role in managing the forests in their traditional areas.

Forestry Products

Many products are made from trees. Trees are the raw materials for these products. **Raw materials** are what we call resources before they are turned into products we use.

Trees are used to make two main kinds of products: lumber products, and pulp and paper products. We usually think of lumber products as wood. Lumber products include different sizes of lumber used for building, as well as plywood, wooden furniture, and cedar shingles for covering walls and roofs. Pulp and paper products include many different kinds of paper, such as the pages in this student book, paper towels, toilet paper, and cardboard.

The flow chart below shows what usually happens to trees after they are logged.

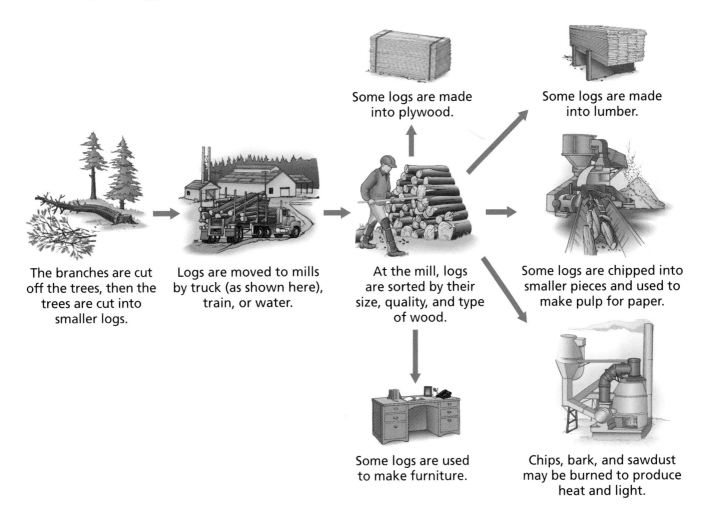

Some logs are made into plywood.

Some logs are made into lumber.

The branches are cut off the trees, then the trees are cut into smaller logs.

Logs are moved to mills by truck (as shown here), train, or water.

At the mill, logs are sorted by their size, quality, and type of wood.

Some logs are chipped into smaller pieces and used to make pulp for paper.

Some logs are used to make furniture.

Chips, bark, and sawdust may be burned to produce heat and light.

⇨ Check Your Understanding

1. How did Aboriginal peoples use forests in the past? How do we use forests today? How are these past and present uses the same? How are they different?

2. Describe two different ways that trees are logged.

3. List two ways that logging has an impact on the local environment. List two things that are being done so that logging has less of an impact on the local environment.

4. List four forest products you have used today.

Awesome SCIENCE

Cedar: The Tree of Life

The Western red cedar is one of the best known and most valuable plants in British Columbia. Cedar trees grow along the coast of British Columbia and in many areas of the interior. They can be 50 to 70 m high and 3 to 6 m wide. In the wild, cedar trees can live for 800 to 1500 years. The wood from cedar trees contains chemicals that keep it from rotting when it is cut.

Long ago, the Aboriginal peoples of British Columbia understood the great value of the cedar tree. They called it "The Tree of Life." Cedar trees provided the coastal Aboriginal peoples with materials for almost every part of their lives. They used the wood from cedars to build longhouses, canoes, and totem poles.

▲ Cedar trees are among the tallest and longest-living trees in Canada.

▲ A longhouse and totem poles in the Haida village of Masset, on Haida Gwaii.

Aboriginal peoples also used the bark for a variety of things. The bark was carefully removed from the trees to do as little damage as possible. The soft inner bark was separated from the thick outer bark. The inner bark was carefully air-dried, cut into strips, and stored for use. The bark strips were made softer by pounding. They could then be woven into baskets, mats, boxes, diapers, hats, belts, ropes, capes, blankets, towels, and many more items used in daily life.

Cedar trees continue to play an important role in the lives of many Aboriginal peoples. They continue to use cedars as they did in the past.

A Look into the Past

Aboriginal peoples saw the cedar as a gift from Earth that needed to be treated with respect and used carefully. A whole tree was cut down only if the entire tree was needed. Many Aboriginal peoples harvested both bark and planks from living cedar trees. This allowed the trees to continue to grow. Trees that were used in this way can still be found in the forests of British Columbia.

▲ The capes the women are wearing and the baskets are traditional uses of cedar bark.

▲ These trees show one of the traditional methods of harvesting cedar trees.

4 Water

In British Columbia, we are lucky to have clean water to use. In many parts of the world, clean water is hard to find, so people use the water very carefully. How carefully do you use water?

Try This

Calculate Your Daily Water Use

Skills Focus: observing, inferring

1. Make a table like the one below

My Water Usage

Activity	Time	Amount of water	Water used
showering	5 minutes	25 L per minute	25 L per minute x 5 minutes = 125 L

2. Keep track of the water you use for one day. Each time you do one of the activities shown below, list it in your table. Include how long you did the activity if needed. At the end of the day, calculate how much water you used, based on the amounts in the table below.

Average Amount of Water for Activities

Activity	Amount of water
using washing machine	230 L per use
running dishwasher	65 L per use
flushing toilet	20 L per use
bathing	130 L per use
showering	25 L per minute
washing hands under tap	12 L per minute

3. In what ways could you reduce how much water you use?

Did you know?

Every person in Canada uses an average of 350 L of water a day. This amount includes about 100 L a day just to flush the toilet.

Where Does Water Come From?

Water is a renewable resource that all living things need to stay alive. Most of the water on Earth is salt water in oceans and seas. The rest is fresh water. About three quarters of the fresh water on Earth is found as ice. This means that only a very small amount of all the water on Earth is fresh and in a liquid form that humans can use.

Fresh water is found in lakes, rivers, streams, ponds, and underground. The supply of fresh water does not decrease when we use it because it is recycled. Water can be used over and over again as it goes through the **water cycle.** In the water cycle, water evaporates, then condenses and falls back to Earth as precipitation. When precipitation falls on land, one of two things happens:

- It runs over the surface of the land into a stream, river, lake, or ocean. This is called **surface runoff.**
- It goes into the ground. This is called **groundwater.** Groundwater supplies water for wells and freshwater springs. Unless groundwater is brought to the surface, it will eventually flow into a stream, lake, or river.

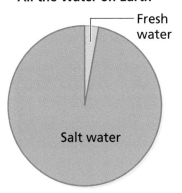

All the Water on Earth

▲ Nearly all the water on Earth is salt water.

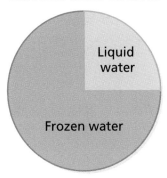

The Fresh Water on Earth

▲ We can use only about one quarter of the fresh water found on Earth.

The Water Cycle

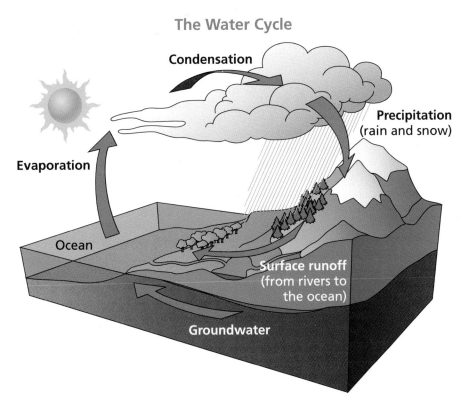

Watersheds

➡ Learning Tip

Check your understanding of the vocabulary words in this section. Take turns explaining them to a partner. Try to use your own words.

A **watershed** is an area of land that drains into a river or lake. When precipitation falls on a watershed, it flows down to the river or lake or it sinks into the ground and becomes groundwater.

As water flows on the surface, it picks up materials such as soil and rocks, and carries these materials to the river or lake.

Groundwater picks up chemicals and materials like soil and rocks and carries them with it as it goes into the ground. This is called **leaching** [LEECH-ing]. Leaching can cause soil pollution. **Soil pollution** happens when chemicals and other harmful substances get into the soil. Things that cause pollution are called pollutants. Some pollutants stay in the soil and may be taken up by plants. Other pollutants are eventually carried to the river or lake.

Watersheds are very important because they usually supply all the water needs and wants for an area.

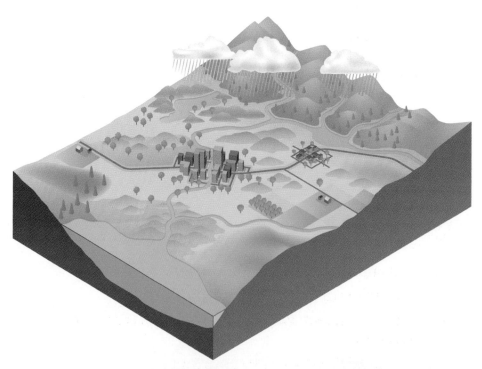

▲ A watershed includes both land and water. Each watershed has its own habitats, such as rivers, streams, farmland, and cities.

Water Pollution

We need clean fresh water for drinking, cooking, washing, swimming, and other uses. Similarly, plants and animals need clean water to live in and drink. Many things, however, can make water polluted. **Water pollution** happens when harmful substances or organisms that can make animals and plants sick get into the water.

Pollutants can get into the water in many ways. Many of the products we use to clean contain pollutants. Some people pour chemicals, such as paint and motor oil, down a drain or on the ground. Body wastes from farm animals can leach into the soil or be washed directly into streams when there is rain. Garbage from landfills can leach directly into the soil. Industries have to follow strict rules to treat the water they use before it goes back into rivers and streams. Some industries, however, may illegally dump pollutants into streams and rivers.

Water usually treated

Water usually treated

Water sometimes treated

Water usually treated

▲ Water is usually treated to make it safe for us to use.

⇨ Check Your Understanding

1. Why is water such an important resource?
2. What is the water cycle? Why is it important?
3. What is a watershed? Why should communities protect their watersheds?
4. How can rivers and lakes become polluted?

5 Design Your Own Experiment

◉ SKILLS MENU

◉ Questioning	◉ Measuring
◉ Predicting	○ Classifying
◉ Designing Experiments	○ Inferring
◉ Fair Testing	◉ Interpreting Data
◉ Observing	◉ Communicating

⇨ Learning Tip

Before you begin this experiment, review Design Your Own Experiment in the Skills Handbook.

How Does Water Pollution Affect Living Things?

Most soaps used to contain chemicals called phosphates [FOSS-fates]. Phosphates helped the soaps clean better. Some of these phosphates, however, caused water pollution when they went down drains into the water supply.

Phosphates that go into the water supply can end up in soil. They can also end up in ponds or streams.

▲ Phosphates help detergents work better, but can cause water pollution when they go down the drain and end up in a stream like this one.

Today, most soaps contain very few phosphates. However, detergents for automatic dishwashers and some other types of detergent contain high amounts of phosphates.

Design an experiment to find out how phosphates affect plant growth. You could water seedlings with a soap-and-water mixture that contains phosphates, then measure their growth. Seedlings are young plants that are just beginning to grow above the soil.

Question

Write a question you would like answered about how phosphates in water affect plant growth. Your question could be similar to one of these:

- Will the amount of phosphates in water affect the growth of seedlings?
- Which seedlings will grow better—ones watered with no phosphates or ones watered with phosphates?

Prediction

Think about how many soap-and-water mixtures you will use and how each mixture will be different. Think about including seedlings that get water only. Predict which mixture will grow seedlings the best.

Materials

Decide what materials you will need to conduct your experiment. Check with your teacher to make sure that these materials are safe for you to use.

Procedure

Design a procedure to test your prediction. A procedure is a step-by-step description of how you will conduct your experiment. It must be clear enough for someone else to follow and do the exact same experiment. Think about

- how many seedlings you will use (Will you use groups of seedlings? How many seedlings will you have in a group?)
- how you will measure the growth of the seedlings (Will you measure the growth of each seedling in a group and find the average growth?)
- how often you will water the seedlings
- what amount of water you will use each time you water the seedlings
- how long your trial will last
- how the soap-and-water mixture you use for each seedling will be different (Will the amount of water be the same, but the amount of soap different? Will you use only water and no soap for one group of seedlings?)

Hand in your procedure, including any safety precautions, to your teacher for approval.

Data and Observations

Create a data table to record your observations as you carry out your experiment. A sample data table is shown below.

	Data Table for Experiment 9.5				
	Seedling group number	Amount of soap in water	Average height of seedlings at beginning of experiment	Average height of seedlings at end of experiment	Other observations
	1				

Interpret Data and Observations

1. Which seedlings grew the most? Which seedlings grew the least?

2. What happened to the colour of the seedlings during the experiment?

3. Do you think the phosphates in the water affected the growth of the seedlings? Why or why not?

4. Look back at your prediction. Did your results fully support, partly support, or not support your prediction? Write a conclusion for your experiment.

Apply and Extend

1. Think about how phosphates affected the growth of the seedlings. What would happen to plants in a pond that contained phosphates? How could this affect other organisms in the pond ecosystem?

2. Why do you think some manufacturers now make soap without phosphates?

⇨ Check Your Understanding

1. What variable did you change in your experiment?
2. What variable did you measure?
3. What variables did you keep the same?
4. Was your experiment a fair test? How do you know?

Renewable Energy Resources

Some renewable resources can be used to produce energy. Water is the most important renewable energy resource in British Columbia.

Water can be used to produce electricity. This is called hydroelectricity. Dams are built on rivers because the water needs to flow quickly downward to produce electricity. Dams hold back the water. The water can then be released when it is needed to produce electricity. British Columbia has many fast-flowing rivers, so many dams have been built. More than three quarters of British Columbia's electricity needs are met by hydroelectricity.

▲ The lake that is created behind a dam is often used for recreation, such as boating.

Hydroelectricity is renewable and does not pollute the water. Building a dam, however, can cause problems. When a dam is built, the area behind the dam fills up with water. This floods land, which can destroy farmland and habitats for wildlife. For example, flooding has destroyed many habitats for some migrating birds who build nests in the area. Before a dam is built, it is important to study the possible effects of the dam on the habitats for wildlife and the surrounding communities.

Energy from the Sun

Scientists are developing other sources of energy that will not cause problems for the environment. One of these sources of energy is solar energy. **Solar energy** is energy that comes from the Sun. Solar energy can be changed into heat or electricity.

▲ Solar panels collect the Sun's heat and use it to produce electricity or heat water.

▲ Solar cells in calculators change light from the Sun into electricity.

Sunlight does not pollute. There is also a never-ending supply of it. Nevertheless, there are many drawbacks to using solar energy. It is only available during the day when the Sun is shining, so solar cells do not work at night. In many parts of the world, such as British Columbia, there is not enough sunlight year-round to make solar energy practical. For these reasons, solar energy is usually used along with other energy resources.

⇨ Check Your Understanding

1. What are renewable energy resources?

2. Explain how hydroelectricity can be good and bad for the environment.

3. Is solar energy a good alternative to hydroelectricity? Why or why not?

Chapter Review

Renewable resources can replace themselves.

Key Idea: We harvest and process renewable resources to meet our needs.

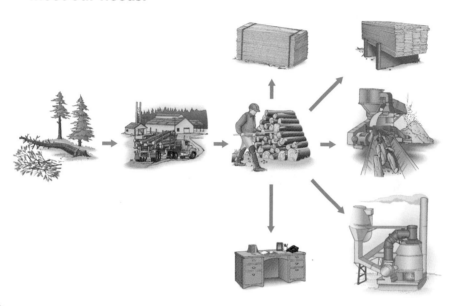

Vocabulary

renewable p. 177

harvesting p. 180

local environment
 p. 185

raw materials p. 186

water cycle p. 191

surface runoff p. 191

groundwater p. 191

watershed p. 192

leaching p. 192

solar energy p. 199

Key Idea: Harvesting and processing renewable resources has an impact on the environment.

Vocabulary

soil pollution p. 192

water pollution
 p. 193

Key Idea: Traditional Aboriginal cultures protect and conserve resources.

Key Idea: We must conserve and protect our renewable resources for future use.

Review Key Ideas and Vocabulary

Use the vocabulary words in your answers to the questions.

1. Choose one renewable resource, and explain why it is considered renewable.

2. How can the methods of harvesting salmon have an effect on whether salmon will be available in the future?

3. How have Aboriginal peoples' traditional practices helped to conserve renewable resources?

4. Why do we process renewable resources?

5. Why must humans make choices about using renewable resources? How can we help to conserve renewable resources?

Apply What You've Learned

Model the Harvesting of a Renewable Resource

Looking Back

You have learned

- that we harvest renewable resources
- why harvesting renewable resources has an impact on the environment
- why we must conserve and protect our renewable resources for the future

In this activity, you will work with a partner to model what can happen to a renewable resource when it is harvested.

Demonstrate Your Learning

Plan and Carry Out Your Modelling Activity

1. Your teacher will give you red beans and white beans to represent trees in a forest. The red beans will be mature trees, and the white beans will be young trees.

2. Start your modelling by placing between 30 and 50 red beans in a bowl. Then add enough white beans to make a forest of 100 trees.

3. Take away beans to show trees being harvested. The beans you take away first will represent Year 1 of harvesting. At the beginning of Year 2, trade 5 white beans for 5 red beans. Also add 4 new white beans. The beans you have after trading and adding beans will be the number you will start with for harvesting in Year 2. Continue harvesting the forest to model 5 or 6 years.

4. Record what happens to the forest in each year that you harvest, for example:

Harvest year	Red beans before harvesting	White beans before harvesting	Red beans harvested	White beans harvested	Red beans at harvest end	White beans at harvest end	Total beans after harvest
Year 1	40	60	20	0	20	60	80
Year 2	20 + 5 = 25	60 − 5 = 55 55 + 4 = 59	15	0	10	59	69

5. Discuss the following questions with your partner.
   • Was there a time when you thought it was all right to harvest the resource? When?
   • Was there a time when you thought it wasn't all right to harvest the resource? When?
   • Did you harvest any young trees? What happened to the resource when you did this?

6. What did you learn about resource use? What would have to happen to maintain a resource? Write a short paragraph about the wise use of resources.

> ⇨ **Assessment Checklist**
>
> **MODELLING**
>
> **As you plan and carry out your activity, make sure that you show you are able to**
>
> ✔ identify the impact of resource harvesting
> ✔ use appropriate scientific words
> ✔ communicate clearly

Non-renewable resources can be used only once.

➡ **Key Ideas**

▸ Most non-renewable resources take millions of years to form.

▸ We extract and process non-renewable resources to meet our needs.

▸ Our use of non-renewable resources has an impact on the environment.

▸ We must make responsible choices when using non-renewable resources.

Can you imagine not having cars? In just 100 years, cars have changed life in Canada. Cars are not like products that are made from renewable resources, such as wood. Cars are mostly made from different metals. Cars also need gasoline to run. We cannot reproduce or re-grow the metals and gasoline for cars.

In this chapter, you will learn about resources, such as metals and gasoline, that are non-renewable. You will learn about the important roles of non-renewable resources in our daily lives—from running cars, planes, trains, and boats to providing the materials used to manufacture many products. You will also learn about the impact of our use of non-renewable resources on the environment. Finally, you will discover why we must make wise choices when using non-renewable resources so that they will be available in the future.

Non-Renewable Resources

Non-renewable [non-rih-NOO-uh-buhl] resources cannot reproduce the way that trees or fish can. They cannot renew themselves like water can through the water cycle. Once non-renewable resources are used, they are considered gone forever.

Model Using a Non-Renewable Resource

Skills Focus: creating models, observing, communicating

1. As a class, form a large circle. Your teacher will give one student a paper bag full of a "resource."

2. Pass the bag around the circle. Take as much or as little of the resource as you want. Stop passing around the bag once it is empty.

3. Did everyone get some of the resource? Why or why not? How do you think this is like Earth's non-renewable resources?

Non-Renewable Resources in British Columbia

There are two types of non-renewable resources: fossil fuels and minerals [MIHN-uhr-uhls]. British Columbia has both types.

Fossil fuels are found under Earth's surface. Coal, oil, and natural gas are examples of fossil fuels that are found in British Columbia. Minerals are materials that naturally occur in rocks. Minerals that are found in British Columbia include copper, gold, silver, and zinc.

British Columbia has many non-renewable resources, including natural gas, coal, and a variety of minerals.

All fossil fuels were formed millions of years ago from the bodies of animals and plant remains. They were all formed in similar ways. For example, coal was formed from huge plants that grew in swampy areas around the world. When the plants died, they sank to the bottoms of the swamps. There, they were broken down by bacteria into a material called peat [PEET]. Over millions of years, layers of mud and soil buried the peat. The layers pressed down on the peat and eventually changed it into coal.

▲ Coal is the product of ancient plants. As they decayed over millions of years, they formed layers of coal deep in Earth.

Coal took millions of years to form. Most minerals we use today were formed millions of years ago. That is why they are both considered non-renewable.

Fossil fuels are used mostly to produce energy. Minerals are used to make many of our everyday products, such as pop cans, baby powder, toothpaste, calcium tablets, pipes and wires, and even money.

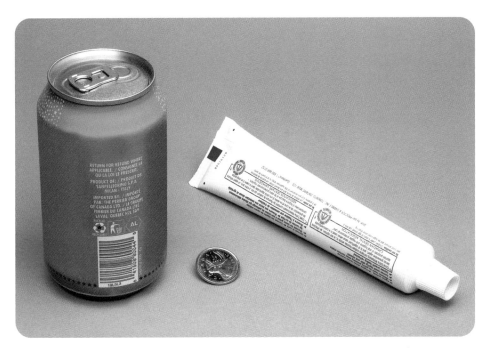

▲ Many everyday objects, such as pop cans, toothpaste, and coins, are made from minerals.

Humans need to make wise choices when using non-renewable resources. Earth has only a limited amount of these resources. Once they are gone, they cannot be replaced.

⇨ **Check Your Understanding**

1. What is a non-renewable resource?
2. Explain how fossil fuels were formed. List the fossil fuels found in British Columbia.
3. List three minerals found in British Columbia. Why are minerals important?

Mining Minerals

Minerals are important to us because we use them in many products in many different ways. For example, graphite [GRAF-ite] is a mineral used to make pencils. Diamonds are a mineral used to make jewellery [JOO-uhl-ree].

▲ The mineral diamond can be used for a variety of purposes. It can be used as a bit for a drill and also in jewellery, such as this ring.

Scientists are always working on new ways to use minerals. Therefore, the list of their uses is always increasing. Perhaps the most useful minerals to us are metals. Metals are found in rocks, like all minerals. Some common metals are gold, silver, and copper.

Rocks that have a lot of minerals in them are called ores. Because most ores are under the surface of Earth, they must be extracted. When something is **extracted,** it is taken out of something else. Ores are taken out of the ground. We usually call this mining.

There are two main ways of extracting minerals from Earth: underground mining and open-pit mining.

Underground Mining

Some minerals are found deep below Earth's surface. To extract these minerals, a mine is dug deep in the ground. Tunnels are built to get to the ore. The ore is usually drilled or blasted loose with explosives. Then the ore is moved to the surface and taken to a mill to be processed. Zinc and silver are two metals that are mined in underground mines in British Columbia.

Underground mining does not destroy large areas of land on the surface. It causes other problems, however. The groundwater that flows through the rocks can be polluted by the mining, and this can pollute water far away from a mine. As well, underground mining is very expensive. It costs a lot of money to build underground tunnels and to move equipment to them. Underground mining is also dangerous. Harmful gases can build up in the tunnels and cause explosions. Workers in many underground mines must wear breathing equipment to protect themselves from breathing in harmful dust and gases.

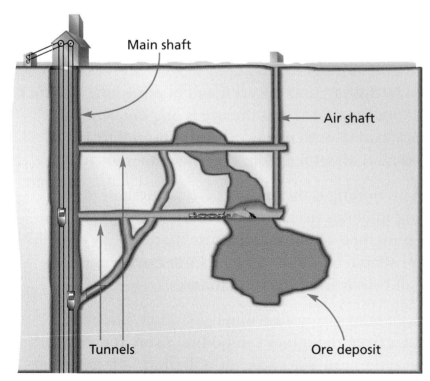

▲ In underground mines, tunnels are built below the surface to get to the ore.

Open-Pit Mining

Open-pit mines are used when minerals are found close to Earth's surface. Copper and gold are metals that are often found close to Earth's surface. They are mined in British Columbia in open-pit mines.

▲ Huckleberry Mine is an open-pit copper mine located near Tahtsa Lake.

In open-pit mining, the top layer of soil and rock is removed by drilling into the rock and blasting away the rock until the ore is found. Then the ore is dug out with large machines, loaded onto trucks, and transported to a mill. The mineral is separated from the ore at the mill.

Open-pit mining is the least expensive method of extracting minerals from Earth. It is also considered to be the safest method of mining, because there are no tunnels that can collapse on mine workers. Ores can be removed quickly and easily from open-pit mines.

Open-pit mines can cause water pollution, however. Wastewater from the mines can pollute rivers and creeks. Open-pit mines can also cause air pollution. **Air pollution** happens when substances that can harm the natural environment are released into the atmosphere.

The air above a specific area is called an **air shed.** An air shed is the air shared by every living thing in an area. In open-pit mining, rock dust, exhaust fumes, and other pollutants are put into the air shed. Look back at the photo of the open-pit mine. What other effects do you think open-pit mining has on the environment?

▲ An air shed can become polluted because of mining and other human activities that release dust and fumes into the air.

⇨ Check Your Understanding

1. Draw a diagram to show how a mineral is extracted from an open-pit mine or an underground mine.

2. In your notebook, make a table like the one below. Then complete your table.

Types of mining	Open-pit mining	Underground mining
Advantages		
Disadvantages		

ScienceWorks

Plants: Nature's Way of Helping the Environment

Every year, we use more of Earth's resources to meet our many wants and needs. This means that our impact on the environment is also growing. In many parts of the world there are shortages of resources, as well as environmental problems such as soil, water, and air pollution.

Scientists are starting to use plants to help repair damage caused by our use of resources, and to help keep our environment healthy.

Cleaning Soil and Water

Scientists are using their knowledge of how plants grow to help clean up soil and water that is polluted with harmful chemicals. They know that as plants take up nutrients and water from the soil, they also take up these chemicals. So they are using common plants like sunflowers, poplar and willow trees, and cabbages to clean up soil and water pollution.

In Chilliwack, British Columbia, scientists are using plants to clean up

▲ Scientists are using plants like sunflowers and poplar trees to clean up polluted water and soil.

lead and copper from a gun-firing range used by the Canadian military. The plants take up the minerals as they grow. Once they are fully grown, the plants are chopped down, and the minerals are disposed of safely.

Trees like willows and poplars are also being used to clean up polluted water and soil. A poplar tree can filter almost 100 L of polluted water a day.

Green Roofs

▲ Green roofs, like this one on the Vancouver Public Library, help clean the air, save energy, and provide a home for birds and insects.

Most people would never think of growing a lawn on the roof, but scientists have found a very good reason for growing lawns and gardens on the roofs of buildings: these roofs help keep the environment healthy.

Green roofs keep buildings warmer in winter and cooler in summer, so less energy is needed to heat and cool them. Green roofs keep the air cleaner by taking in harmful gases, dust, and other pollutants in the air, and by putting out oxygen. Green roofs also add green space to a community that attracts birds and insects, and can be used to grow food.

Making "Plastic" from Plants

Scientists have discovered another important use for plants—plants can replace plastic in many products. Plastic is lightweight, strong, and cheap, but it is not biodegradable. It takes hundreds of years to break down and return to Earth. Also, the chemicals used in making plastics can pollute the air, water, and soil.

Now scientists are using material from corn, wheat, palm trees, and other common plants to replace some plastic products. Already, inventors have created plant-based grocery bags, disposable dishes, packaging, and disposable diapers. After it is used, a product made from plants can be thrown into a compost pile. The compost can be used as a fertilizer to help grow more plants.

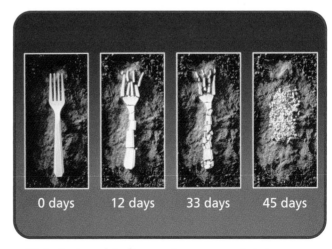

0 days   12 days   33 days   45 days

▲ This fork made from plant materials becomes compost in about 45 days.

Processing Ore to Find Minerals

Once the ore is brought to the surface, the next step is to separate the mineral from the rest of it. The process for separating the mineral always begins with crushing the ore. Then different methods are used to get the pure mineral. No matter what method is used, there will be waste left over, like ground rock, other non-valuable minerals, and chemicals.

Much of the ground rock and non-valuable minerals are put back into the ground. A lot of the water and chemicals used in the processing of ore are recycled so they can be used again. The rest of the waste rock and liquid waste are called tailings. Tailings are placed in tailings ponds.

The waste in tailings ponds can be harmful to people and the surrounding environment, so the ponds are lined with clay or plastic. This stops the wastes from escaping into streams, lakes, and groundwater.

▲ This tailings pond is lined with a mixture of clay and sand to prevent leaching.

Processing Copper

Copper is usually mined in open-pit mines. The extracted ore usually contains very small amounts of copper. The following diagram shows one way copper ore is processed to get the copper.

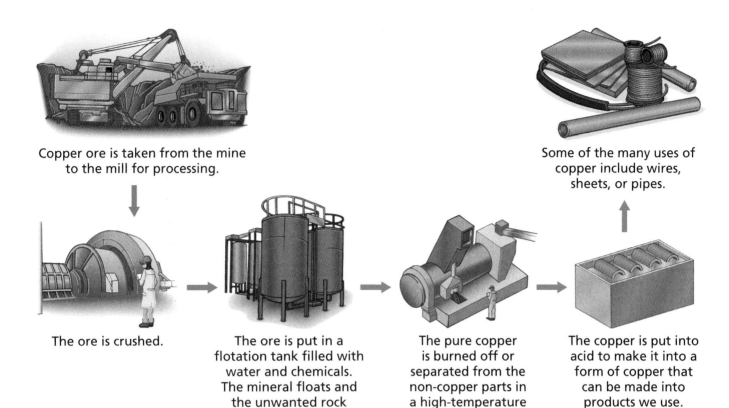

Copper ore is taken from the mine to the mill for processing.

The ore is crushed.

The ore is put in a flotation tank filled with water and chemicals. The mineral floats and the unwanted rock (tailings) sinks.

The pure copper is burned off or separated from the non-copper parts in a high-temperature furnace.

The copper is put into acid to make it into a form of copper that can be made into products we use.

Some of the many uses of copper include wires, sheets, or pipes.

▲ Copper ore is processed into copper that can be used to make many products.

Processed copper is sold to different manufacturers, who use it as the raw material for many products. For example, copper can be made into wires that are used to conduct electricity. It can also be flattened into sheets. These sheets can be used to cover the roofs of large buildings. Copper can be made into pipes, as well. The copper products are sent to different stores, where they are sold.

⇨ Check Your Understanding

1. When processing ore, what is done to protect the environment? What is done to conserve resources?

2. In your own words, explain one way copper is processed.

Chapter 10

4 Opening and Closing a Mine

⇨ Learning Tip

Make connections to other things you have learned about in school. Have you learned about decision-making in Social Studies? How does good decision-making work?

A mine is not opened as soon as ore is discovered. There are many things to think about before a mine is built. The mining company has to decide whether or not the mine will make money. If the mine will not make money, then it will not be built. The company also thinks about the safety of workers.

Opening a Mine

Before a mine opens, scientists, environmentalists, politicians, and community members study what impact the mine will have. They carefully consider the type of mining needed to remove the ore. They also consider how the mine will affect the living and non-living things in the environment—the people, animals, plants, land, water, and air. As well, they consider how materials will be transported to and from the mine, where workers will live, and what to do with the wastes from the mining process. If the effects on the environment will be greater than the benefits from the mine, then the mineral may not be mined.

▲ What do you think would happen to this environment if an open-pit mine was built?

216

Closing a Mine

Minerals are non-renewable so, over time, they run out and mines are closed. Today, before a mine is even opened, people think about what will happen when the mine is closed. The land used for mining needs to be returned to a usable environment for living things. The process of doing this is called reclamation [rek-luh-MAY-shun].

There are many things that can be done to reclaim an open-pit mine. The tailings are treated if they are harmful to the environment. Dried tailings can then be used to fill the pit, along with the rocks and soil that were removed when the pit was dug. Sometimes the tailings are piled up in rows, covered with soil, and planted with plants that normally grow in the area. If the rocks and soil that were removed to dig the pit are not used to fill the pit, they can also be piled up, covered with soil, and planted.

▲ Reclaimed tailings at Fording River Mine, Elk Valley Coal.

The pit is not always filled with tailings or rocks and soil. Sometimes, it is allowed to fill with rainwater and snow. This creates a pond.

▲ The top photo shows the Island Copper Mine when the mine was in use. The bottom photo shows the same mine, once the land was reclaimed. The pit was turned into a lake using sea water.

⇨ Check Your Understanding

1. Name three things that have to be considered before a mine is built.

2. What is reclamation? Describe two things that might be done to reclaim an open-pit mine.

Conduct an Investigation

SKILLS MENU

○ Questioning	○ Measuring
○ Predicting	○ Classifying
○ Designing Experiments	● Inferring
	● Interpreting Data
○ Fair Testing	
● Observing	● Communicating

Mining Chocolate Chips

There are many things to think about before a mine is opened. One thing that mining companies think about is whether or not a mine can make money. Mining companies also think about questions like these:

- Is there a large enough amount of the mineral? If there isn't enough of the mineral in the ore, the company may not get the money back that it would have to pay to start and run the mine.
- How expensive will the equipment be? The company might consider how difficult it will be to get the ore out of the ground. The company might need to buy more or bigger pieces of equipment if the mining will be difficult.
- How much will it cost to reclaim the land after the mine is closed? One thing the company might consider is how large an area the mine will cover. The larger the area, the higher the cost will be to reclaim the land.

In this investigation, you will operate a chocolate chip mine and try to make money.

chocolate chip cookies

Question

Can you open and operate a chocolate chip mine that makes money?

Materials

- 3 different brands of chocolate chip cookies
- sheet of graph paper: 100 squares to the page
- small pile of round toothpicks
- small pile of flat toothpicks
- small pile of paper clips
- stopwatch or clock with second hand

graph paper

round toothpicks   flat toothpicks

paper clips

stopwatch

Step 1 Work with a partner. In your notebook, make a table like the one below. You will have $20 when you start up your mine.

Data Table for Investigation 10.5							
Original amount of money	Cost of property	Size of property	Cost of equipment	Cost of operating mine	Number of chips mined	Value of chips	Environmental impact to land and cost of reclamation
$20							

Step 2 Go to your teacher and buy one of the three properties (chocolate chip cookies) that can be mined. Property A costs $3, Property B costs $5, and Property C costs $7. Record the cost in your table.

Step 3 Place your property on a sheet of graph paper and trace it. Count the number of squares that your cookie covers. (Count partly covered squares as full squares.) Record this number in your table.

Step 4 Buy your mining equipment. You can buy more than one piece of equipment, but you cannot share any equipment with other groups. A flat toothpick costs $2, a round toothpick costs $4, and a paper clip costs $6. If a piece of equipment breaks, you must buy a new piece. Record the cost of your equipment in your table.

Step 5 You will have 5 minutes to operate your mine. The cost will be $5. Record this cost in your table.

Step 6 Use your equipment to "mine" your chocolate chips. The cookie must stay on the graph paper. You can use only your own equipment to mine the chips.

Step 7 Count the number of chocolate chips you mined. Count full chips and half chips. You can put smaller pieces together to make whole or half chips. Record the total number of chips in your table.

Step 8 Whole chips are worth $2, and half chips are worth $1. How much are your mined chips worth? Record their value in your table. This will be the amount of money your mine made.

Step 9 Your mine will have an environmental impact on the land. You will need to pay to reclaim the land your mine used. The cost of reclaiming each square of land covered by your mine will be 5¢. Calculate the cost of reclamation and record this in your table.

Interpret Data and Observations

1. Add up all the costs of your mine—property, equipment, operating, and reclamation. Subtract this amount from your original $20. Then add the value of your mined chocolate chips. Did your mine make any money?

2. Suggest ways to improve the operation of your mine. Would you buy a different property? Would you change the equipment you used? Be specific in your answer.

Apply and Extend

1. Make a list of all the expenses (things that cost money) that a company would have to consider when operating a mine. Which costs did you consider in this investigation?

2. What else would a company have to consider when operating a mine?

⇨ Check Your Understanding

1. Give an example of how working with a partner improved this investigation.

The Pros and Cons of a New Copper Mine

Learning Tip

Before you begin this activity, read Explore an Issue in the Skills Handbook.

Mining is an important part of the economy in British Columbia. Mining provides jobs and earns money for both mining communities and the province. Mining changes the way the land is used, however. As a result, it can affect the local environment and cause pollution. In this activity, you will work in a group to explore the issue of whether a mine should be allowed to open. Then you will reach a decision about the issue as a class.

The Issue

A mining company has found copper ore in your area. The ore is near the surface, so the company has asked the government for permission to build an open-pit mine. There are a lot of people in the town without jobs, so these people would welcome the mine. The local Aboriginal community is concerned, however, that chemicals used in the mine would hurt fish and other animals, and that the water supply could be contaminated. Also, some people from a nearby town are concerned that the mine would ruin the natural beauty of the area. This would result in fewer tourists visiting local hotels, restaurants, and other businesses.

The mining company has said that it would restore the land once the mine closed. People opposed to the mine say that this would be too late. They have asked the government to turn down the mining company's request.

Identify Perspectives

Work in a group of four or five. Your group will represent a group of people who will be affected by the mine. For example, your group could represent one of the following groups:

- the mining company
- the Aboriginal community
- the town council
- people from the town who want jobs
- a nearby company that needs the copper to make products to sell
- scientists who are concerned about the impact of the mine on the local environment

After you have chosen the group you will represent, think about the viewpoint of this group. You may want to do some research in a library or on the Internet to learn about similar situations. What reasons did different people give for supporting or opposing a mine? As a group, decide whether or not you will support the mine. Write a list of reasons for your viewpoint.

Make a Decision

Present your viewpoint to the class, along with your reasons. After all the groups have presented their viewpoints, discuss the different viewpoints as a class. Decide whether the class is for or against the mine. You could take a vote to find out whether the majority of students are for or against the mine.

Communicate Your Decision

With your group, write a letter to a local newspaper summarizing your viewpoint on the issue. In your letter, also describe how you felt about the class decision. Did you think it was fair? Why or why not?

⇨ Check Your Understanding

1. Why do you think it is important to consider different viewpoints on an issue?

chapter 70

7 *Fossil Fuels*

We depend on fossil fuels for most of our energy needs. Many homes and buildings are heated by oil or natural gas. Cars, buses, and planes need oil and gas to run. As well, fossil fuels earn money for British Columbia.

British Columbia has large supplies of natural gas and coal, but only small amounts of oil.

▲ Fossil fuels are used to heat homes and run cars.

Coal

The most important fossil fuel for British Columbia is coal. British Columbia produces about one third of all the coal in Canada. Since British Columbia also produces a lot of hydroelectricity, only a small amount of the coal is used to meet British Columbia's energy needs. Instead, the coal is sent to many parts of the world, where it is burned to produce electricity and to make steel and other products.

▲ Coal from British Columbia is shipped to many parts of the world.

Coal needs to be mined. As you have learned, mining has many impacts on the environment. Burning coal also has environmental impacts. Burning coal releases pollutants into the air. These pollutants can be harmful to humans, animals, plants, and the atmosphere of Earth.

Natural Gas and Oil

Natural gas is a gas that is burned to heat homes and businesses and to supply power to some cars and buses. Oil is used to run cars, buses, trucks, and planes. It can also be used to heat buildings.

Both natural gas and oil deposits are found deep beneath the surface of Earth. Wells are drilled to get to these deposits. The oil and gas are pumped to the surface and then transported in large pipelines. Drilling and building wells and pipelines can disturb the environment.

Burning natural gas is cleaner than burning coal because natural gas does not produce as many pollutants. Natural gas, however, does produce small amounts of some pollutants. Burning oil causes less damage to the environment than burning coal, but it causes more damage than burning natural gas.

Both oil and natural gas are extracted on land or in the ocean. When oil or natural gas wells are set up in the ocean, they are called offshore rigs. There are several offshore oil rigs in Canada, such as Hibernia off the coast of Newfoundland.

▲ What environmental impacts do you think oil rigs like this one could have?

⟐ Learning Tip

As you read, make personal connections. How do you use fossil fuels in your daily life? How can you help conserve them?

Fossil fuels are the main source of energy in Canada and around the world. Producing and using fossil fuels has great impacts on the environment. As well, fossil fuels are being used up at a fast rate. To stop the damage that fossil fuels cause to the environment, scientists are working hard to develop new energy sources that do not pollute and are renewable. Until new energy sources are ready to replace fossil fuels, however, we must learn how to conserve them.

⟐ Check Your Understanding

1. Why are fossil fuels important to British Columbians?
2. Describe two impacts of fossil fuels on the environment.
3. Why do we need to find new sources of energy?

Tech·CONNECT

Designing Better Cars

Most people love cars. Cars make our daily lives so easy that it is hard to imagine not having cars. Our love of cars has two big problems, however:

- Cars run on gasoline, which is made from oil. Oil is a non-renewable resource. As more people drive, and drive more, the world's oil supply will shrink.

- Cars put out exhaust, which pollutes the air.

Scientists and engineers have built new types of cars that do not have the same problems. These cars use less gasoline, pollute less, or run on renewable resources. Some of these cars are for sale now, while others are still being developed. One day, you may drive a car like one of these.

▲ This hybrid car runs on both gasoline and electricity.

▲ This little three-wheeled car runs on electricity only, so it doesn't pollute. It can go as fast as 110 kilometres per hour (km/h). It is also much lighter than most cars on the road today.

▲ This car of the future has extra large wheels. It will need less energy to run than cars with regular sized wheels.

Chapter Review

Non-renewable resources can be used only once

Key Idea: Most non-renewable resources take millions of years to form.

Vocabulary

non-renewable
p. 205

Key Idea: We extract and process non-renewable resources to meet our needs.

Vocabulary

extracted p. 208

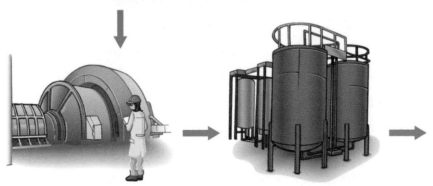

Key Idea: Our use of non-renewable resources has an impact on the environment.

Vocabulary
air pollution p. 210
air shed p. 211

Key Idea: We must make responsible choices when using non-renewable resources.

Review Key Ideas and Vocabulary

Use the vocabulary words in your answers to the questions.

1. What are non-renewable resources? Give an example of a non-renewable resource, and explain how it is formed.

2. What are the two types of non-renewable resources that are found in British Columbia? Name one use for each resource.

3. Describe one way to extract a non-renewable resource from Earth. What are the environmental impacts of extracting this resource?

4. Should one person or group make a decision about mining or drilling for a non-renewable resource? Why or why not?

Apply What You've Learned

Research a Local Non-Renewable Resource

Looking Back

You have learned

- how non-renewable resources are extracted and processed
- that extracting and processing non-renewable resources has an impact on the environment
- why we must conserve and protect our non-renewable resources for the future

In this activity, you will choose and research a local non-renewable resource or a product that is made by processing a non-renewable resource. You will then choose a way to present what you learned from your research.

Demonstrate Your Learning

Research a Resource and Present the Information

1. **Choose a topic.** With your class, brainstorm a list of non-renewable resources that are found in your community and products that are made from non-renewable resources. Then, with a partner, choose a topic to research.

2. **Identify the information that you need.** Make a list of what you want to find out about your topic. Your list could include

- how the resource is extracted or processed
- the positive and negative impacts of extracting or processing the resource on the environment and your community
- how the resource is being conserved

3. **Find sources of information.** Identify all the possible sources of information about your topic. These sources might include books, magazines, Internet sites, videotapes, and/or people in your community.

4. **Record the information.** Identify categories or headings for your notes. Record the information you find in your own words. Include notes about drawings or pictures you might use.

5. **Decide how to present your information.** You might write an article, give an oral report, create a display or model, or make a flow chart.

Present your information to the class.

⇨ Assessment Checklist

RESEARCH

As you look for and record information, make sure that you show you are able to

- identify the scientific information you need to find out
- choose and record useful information from different sources
- organize your information

PRESENTATION

As you prepare your presentation, make sure that you show you are able to

- include accurate facts
- use appropriate scientific words
- communicate clearly

Design a Plan for Future Resource Use

Looking Back

In this unit, you have learned

- that Earth provides us with natural resources
- that renewable resources can be living or non-living and can be reused
- why non-renewable resources can only be used once
- that our use of resources has an impact on the environment
- why all people should conserve resources

In this activity, you will use your understanding of resource use to design a plan for conserving a resource for the future.

Demonstrate Your Learning

Plan

1. Choose a resource that may disappear from Earth or may become unusable as a resource. The resource can be renewable or non-renewable.

2. Research the uses of the resource you chose. Research how harvesting or extracting the resource affects the environment. If your resource is renewable, how is it renewed? How and why is the resource threatened?

3. Think about the many uses of the resource. How could the resource be conserved so that it will be available for future uses?

Design

1. Draw a full-page sketch for a poster about future uses of the resource. Your sketch should show, in words and pictures, how the resource can be conserved.

2. Share your sketch with at least one other classmate. Ask for feedback. Make any necessary changes and improvements to your sketch based on the feedback.

3. Complete your final poster.

Communicate

1. Present your poster to the class. Include the following information in your presentation:
   - the resource you chose and the reasons for your choice
   - how the resource has been harvested or extracted and how this affects the resource and the environment
   - how your plan will conserve the resource and lessen the environmental impacts of harvesting, extracting, or processing it

⇨ Assessment Checklist

POSTER AND PRESENTATION

Your poster and presentation should show that you are able to
- identify a resource that will be needed in the future
- identify ways that the resource has been harvested or extracted and the impact on the environment
- identify ways that the resource can be conserved
- create a final poster that makes use of the feedback from your classmate(s)

Science Safety Rules

- **Follow your teacher's directions.**

Always follow your teacher's instructions. Ask your teacher for help if you're not sure what to do. Wear safety goggles or other safety equipment that your teacher tells you to wear.

- **Tell your teacher about any problems.**

Tell your teacher immediately if you see a safety hazard, such as broken glass or a spill. Also tell your teacher if you see another student doing something you think is dangerous. Tell your teacher about any allergies or medical problems you have.

- **Be clean and tidy.**

Keep yourself and your work area tidy and clean. Clean up and put away equipment after you have finished. Wash your hands carefully with soap and water at the end of each activity.

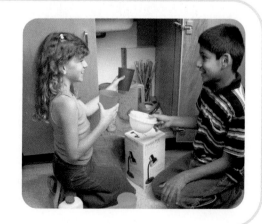

Heat and Fire

- Keep yourself and anything else that can burn away from heat or flames.
- Never touch an object that has been heated. Slowly bring the back of your hand toward the object until you are sure it is not hot.

Chemicals

- Never put your nose directly over a chemical to smell it. Gently wave your hand over the chemical until you can smell the fumes.
- Wash your hands well after handling chemicals.

Handle with Care

Glass and Sharp Objects

- Handle glassware, knives, and other sharp instruments with care.
- Never point a knife or sharp object at another person.
- Tell your teacher immediately if you break glassware or cut yourself.

Living Things

- Treat all living things with care and respect.
- Never hurt an animal in any way.
- Always wash your hands with soap after touching plants or animals.

Conduct an Investigation

When you conduct an investigation or design an experiment, you use many skills. Use this section when you have questions about how to use any of the investigation skills and processes listed here.

Questioning

Scientific investigations start with good questions. To write a good question, you must first decide what you want to know. Good questions often start in one of the following ways:

What causes ...?

How does ... affect ...?

What would happen if ...?

▲ To develop a good question, think carefully about what information you want to find out.

Predicting

When you make a prediction, you state what you think will happen based on what you already know. Scientists do the same thing. They look at data they have gathered to help them see what might happen next or in a similar situation. This is how meteorologists come up with weather forecasts.

Remember that predictions are not guesses. You must be able to give reasons for your predictions. You must also be able to test them by doing experiments.

Fair Testing

When you do an experiment, it is important to think about the things that could affect your results. Things that can affect the results of a test are called variables. To make sure that you are doing a fair test, you have to make sure that you change only one variable at a time. Each time the test is conducted is called a trial.

For example, suppose you wanted to know if your sense of smell affects your sense of taste. You design an experiment to test a student who will wear a blindfold and a noseclip. In your first trial, you give the student a slice of apple to see if the student can identify the taste. You then repeat the procedure, but this time without the noseclip.

In your second trial, the only thing you changed was the noseclip. Everything else stayed the same. The student you used, the type of food, and the blindfold were the same in each trial. Changing any of these variables would affect your results.

To make sure a test is fair, ask yourself these questions:

- Are you changing only one variable at a time?
- Are you observing the same things each time?
- Could any other variable be affecting the results?
- Could other people repeat the experiment and get the same results?

Observing

When you observe something, you use your senses to learn about the world around you. You can also use tools, such as a clock, a tape measure, or a spring scale.

Some observations can be measured. For example, you can measure time, distance, or temperature.

Other observations can't be measured. For example, you can describe the shape, colour, or smell of something, but you cannot measure these observations.

◀ You can describe the shape and colour of this box. You can measure its length, width, and height.

▲ Make sure to measure carefully so you know your observations are accurate.

Measuring

Measuring is an important part of observation. When you measure an object, you can describe it exactly. To learn about using measuring tools, turn to "Measuring" on page 244.

Classifying

You classify things when you sort them into groups. When you sort clothes, sporting equipment, or books, you are using a classification system. Scientists use classification the same way. They try to group things that are alike in order to understand the nature of life.

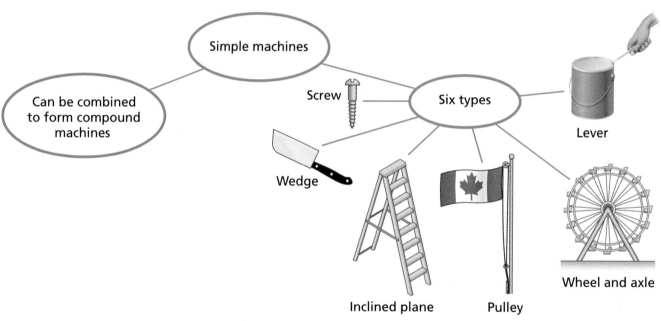

▲ Simple machines are classified into six groups.

Inferring

An inference is a possible explanation of something you observe.

When you make an inference, you are making a "best guess." An observation, on the other hand, is based on what you discover with your senses and measuring tools. If you say that you heard a dog barking, you are making an observation. If you say that it must be your neighbour's dog, you are making an inference. It may turn out to be someone else's dog.

Interpreting Data

When you interpret data from an investigation, you make sense of it. You look at the measurements you have made to see if they help explain your results. Once you have interpreted your data, you can tell if your prediction is correct.

Often, making tables or graphs of your data will help you see patterns and relationships more easily. Turn to "Communicating Using Tables and Graphs" on page 250 to learn more about creating data tables and graphing your results.

Trial	Where ruler caught (cm)	Reaction time (seconds)
1	25	0.23
2	25	0.23
3	25	0.23
4	20	0.20
5	20	0.20

Communicating

Scientists learn from each other by sharing their observations and conclusions. They present their data in charts, tables, or graphs and in written reports. In this student book, each investigation tells you how to prepare and present your results.

Design Your Own Experiment

Refer to this section when you are designing your own experiment.

Ask a Testable Question

↓

Make a Prediction

↓

Plan the Experiment

↓

List the Materials

↓

Write a Procedure

↓

Record Data and Observations

↓

Interpret Data and Observations

↓

Make a Conclusion

↓

Apply Findings

▲ After observing the difference between his lunch and Dal's, Simon wondered why his food was not as fresh as Dal's.

Scientists design experiments to test their ideas about the things they observe. They follow the same steps you will follow when you design an experiment.

Ask a Testable Question

The first thing you need is a testable question. A testable question is a question that you can answer by conducting a test. What question do you think Simon, in the picture above, would ask?

Make a Prediction

Next, use your past experiences and observations to make a prediction. Your prediction should provide an answer to your question and briefly explain why you think the answer is correct. It should be testable through an experiment. What do you think Simon's prediction would be? Turn to "Predicting" on page 236 to learn more about making a prediction.

Plan the Experiment

Now you need to plan how you will conduct your experiment. Remember that your experiment must be a fair test. Also remember that you must change only one variable at a time. Turn to "Fair Testing" on page 236 to learn about fair tests and variables.

List the Materials

Make a list of all the materials you will need to conduct your experiment. Your list must include the amount and the sizes of any materials you need. As well, you should draw a diagram to show how you will set up the equipment. What materials would Simon need to complete his experiment?

Write a Procedure

The procedure is a step-by-step description of how you will perform your experiment. It must be clear enough for someone else to follow exactly. As well, it must include any safety precautions. Your teacher must approve your procedure and list of materials. What steps and safety precautions should Simon include?

Record Data and Observations

You need to make careful observations so that you can be sure about the effects of the variable you changed. Record your observations, in a data table, chart, or graph. How would Simon record his observations?

Turn to "Observing" on page 237 to read about making observations. Turn to "Creating Data Tables" on page 250 to read about creating data tables.

Interpret Data and Observations

If your experiment is a fair test, you can use your observations to determine the effects of the variable you changed. Scientists often conduct the same test several times to make sure that their observations are accurate.

Make a Conclusion

When you have analyzed your observations, you can use the results to answer your question and determine if your prediction was correct. You can feel confident about your conclusion if your experiment was a fair test.

Apply Findings

The results of scientific experiments add to our knowledge about the world. For example, the results may be applied to develop new technologies and medicines, which help to improve our lives. How do you think Simon could use what he discovered?

Explore an Issue

Use this section when you are doing an "Explore an Issue" activity.

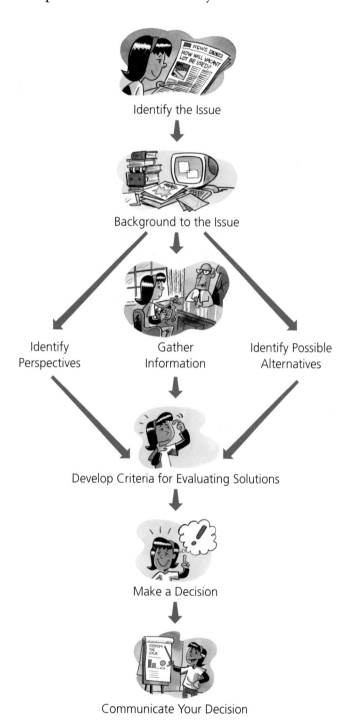

Identify the Issue

Background to the Issue

Identify Perspectives

Gather Information

Identify Possible Alternatives

Develop Criteria for Evaluating Solutions

Make a Decision

Communicate Your Decision

You make decisions every day that can affect yourself, others, and the environment. What is the right decision for you may not work for other people. For example, you might think that bicycles are the only means of transportation that people need. But many people depend on their cars and could not replace them with bicycles.

When a decision has an impact on many people or on the environment, it is important to explore the issue carefully. This means thinking about all the possible solutions and trying to understand all the different points of view—not just your own point of view. It also means researching and investigating your ideas, and talking to and listening to others.

Identify the Issue

The first step in exploring an issue is to identify what the issue is. An issue has more than one solution, and there are different points of view about which solution is the best. Try stating the issue as a question: "What should ...?"

Background to the Issue

The background to the issue is all the information that needs to be gathered and considered before a decision can be made.

- *Identify perspectives.* There are always different points of view on an issue. That's what makes it an issue. For example, suppose that the house at the end of your street has been torn down. The land is owned by the city, and they are deciding what to do with it. People in the neighbourhood want a park to be put in. A house builder wants to build an apartment building.

- *Gather information.* The decision you reach must be based on a good understanding of the issue. You must be in a position to choose the most appropriate solution. To do this, you need to gather facts that represent the different points of view. Watch out for information presenting only one side of the issue. Develop good questions and a plan for your research. Your research may include talking to people, reading about the issue, and doing Internet research. For the land-use issue, you may also want to visit the site to make observations.

- *Identify possible alternatives.* After identifying points of view and gathering information, you can now make a list of possible solutions. You might, for example, come up with the following solutions for the land-use issue:
  - Turn the land into a park.
  - Build an apartment building, so more people can move to the neighbourhood.
  - Create a combination park and small apartment building.

Develop Criteria for Evaluating Solutions

Develop criteria to evaluate each possible solution. For example, should the solution be the one that has the most community support? Should it be the one that protects the environment? You need to decide which criteria you will use to evaluate the solutions so that you can decide which solution is the best.

Make a Decision

This is the stage where everyone gets a chance to share his or her ideas and the information he or she gathered about the issue. Then the group needs to evaluate all the possible solutions and decide on one solution based on the list of criteria.

Communicate Your Decision

Choose a method to communicate your decision. For example, you could choose one of the following methods:

- Write a report.
- Give an oral presentation.
- Design a poster.
- Prepare a slide show.
- Organize a panel presentation.
- Write a newspaper article.

Measuring

Measuring is an important part of doing science. Measurements allow you to give exact information when you are describing something.

Measuring Length

You measure length when you want to find out how long something is. You also measure length when you want to know how deep, how tall, how far, or how wide something is. The metre (m) is the basic unit of length.

> Length is the distance between two points. Four units can be used to measure length: metres (m), centimetres (cm), millimetres (mm), and kilometres (km).
>
> 1000 mm = 1 m   100 cm = 1 m   1000 m = 1 km

Metric ruler

Tape measure

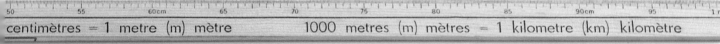

Metre stick

▲ Which of these measuring tools would you use to measure your height? Which would you use to measure the size of your waist? Which would you use to measure the width of your notebook?

Measuring Liquid Volume

You measure volume when you want to measure the amount of liquid in a container. Scientists use special containers, with measurements marked on them, so that they can get precise measures of volume.

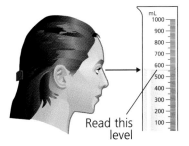

▲ To read the measurement of a liquid correctly, make sure your eyes are at the same level as the top of the liquid.

Volume is the amount of space something takes up. Liquid volume is measured in litres (L) and millilitres (mL).

1000 mL = 1 L

Measuring Temperature

Temperature tells us how hot or cold something is. In science, temperature is measured in degrees Celsius (°C).

0 °C = freezing point of water
20 °C = room temperature
37.6 °C = normal body temperature
100 °C = boiling point of water

There are many different kinds of thermometers, and many work the same way. When the liquid in the thermometer gets warmer, it takes up more space and rises up the tube. When the liquid gets cooler, it shrinks and the liquid goes down. The numbers on thermometers are called the scale. To find the temperature, you read the number on the scale that is at the same height as the liquid.

▲ Hold the thermometer at eye level to be sure your reading is accurate.

Reading for Information

Reading Tips

When you are reading a science textbook, you are reading for information. Reading for information takes some special skills you don't use when you read a story. Here are some tips to help you read.

Before Reading

Look at the pictures and the headings. Ask yourself what the section is going to be about. Think about what you already know about the topic. What else would you like to find out? Write your ideas and questions before you start reading.

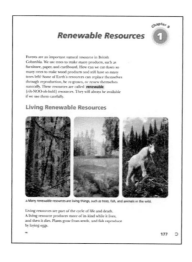

During Reading

Stop and think as you read. Sometimes, you may need to read a part again. Check to make sure you understand. Notice the important science words. Remember, you can use the glossary or study the pictures to help you understand the words. Spend time on the pictures and tables as well as on the words.

After Reading

Ask yourself: What did I learn? What's most important for me to remember? How does this information fit in with other things I already know about? Then, answer the questions at the end of a section. These questions will help you check your understanding of what you read. They will help you make connections to other science topics, to your own life, and to events in Canada and the world.

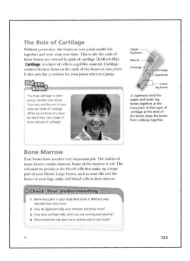

Using Graphic Organizers

Sometimes it is helpful to use a picture or a chart to show what you are thinking. You can read the information in the picture or in the chart just like you read text on a page.

▶ A **word web** shows connections among the different words related to a science topic.

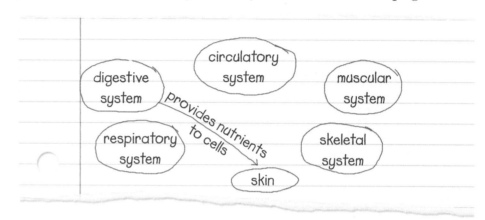

▶ A **KWL chart** shows what you Know about a topic, what you Wonder, and what you have Learned about the topic.

Know	Wonder	Learned
There are many natural resources	Are all natural resources renewable?	Resources can be renewable or non-renewable.

▶ A **flow chart** shows the steps in a process. This diagram shows the steps in digesting an apple.

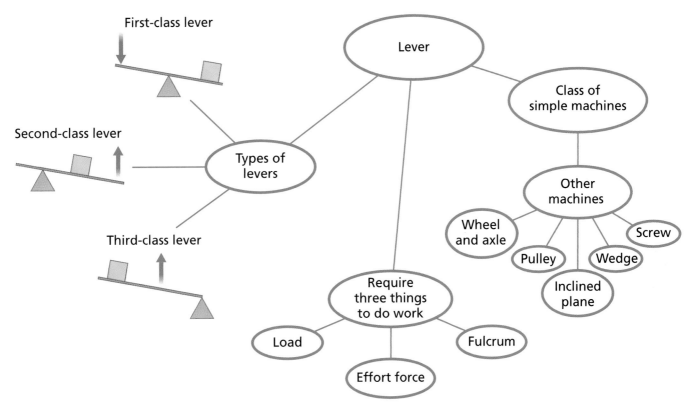

▲ A **concept map** shows a collection of words or pictures or both.

Living and Non-Living Resources

Living resources	Non-living resources
plants	water
animals	wind
	gold

◄ A **T-chart** shows two sides of a topic.

Communicating Using Tables and Graphs

Trial	Where ruler caught (cm)	Reaction time (seconds)
1		
2		
3		
4		
5		

Creating Data Tables

You use data tables to record your observations. Data is the information you collected. In the table on the left, the data is the length the ruler was dropped and the time it took to catch the ruler. Data tables are a good way to organize your information.

Graphing Data

Sometimes you can create graphs from the data you collect. When you graph data, you show the patterns or relationships in the data. Graphs make the information easier to see. Different types of graphs show different information.

Bar Graphs

A **bar graph** shows relationships between separate sets of data. It is a way to show data that uses horizontal or vertical bars. Bar graphs are useful when you want to compare data. Look at the bar graph here. It shows the amount of water used for different activities.

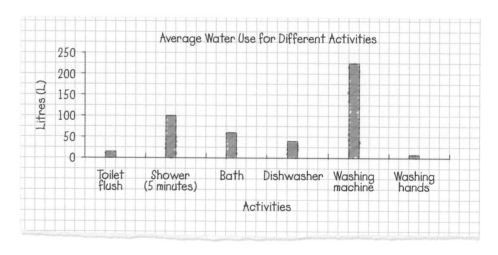

Line Graphs

A **line graph** shows changes in measurement over time. A line graph is useful when you are looking at a relationship between two different things. The line graph for the data here shows the amount of fish caught in British Columbia from 1976 to 2003.

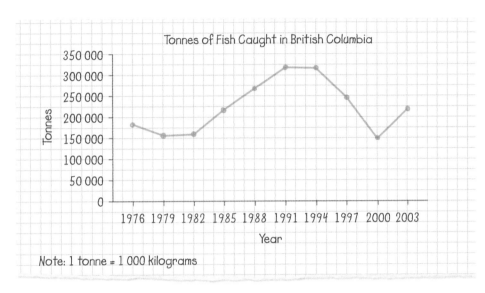

Note: 1 tonne = 1 000 kilograms

Circle Graphs

A **circle graph** (or pie graph) shows the whole of something divided into all its parts. A circle graph is round and compares data by showing it as parts of the circle. This circle graph shows favourite sports of students in a class.

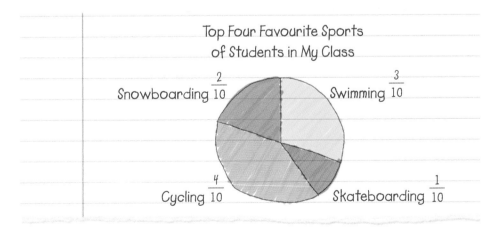

Glossary

A

air pollution the state of air that has been made unclean by harmful substances

air shed the air above a specific area; the air shared by every living thing in the area

arteries thick blood vessels that carry blood away from your heart; this blood usually carries oxygen

axle the rod part of a wheel and axle (a simple machine)

B

balanced forces two forces of equal strength that are acting in opposite directions on an object; when forces are balanced, the motion of the object does not change

biodegradable made from materials that were once living; biodegradable products can be broken down by organisms

bladder a balloon-like organ that holds urine until it is released from your body

blood cells the solid parts of your blood; there are three kinds of blood cells: red blood cells, white blood cells, and platelets

blood vessels hollow tubes that contain your blood; your blood moves through your body in blood vessels

bones pieces that form your skeleton, which gives shape and support to your body and protects your internal organs

brain an organ inside your skull, made from nerve cells; it receives messages from all parts of your body and sends out messages in return

C

carbon dioxide a gas produced by your cells when they produce energy; you get rid of it by breathing it out through your lungs

cartilage a layer of cells in a gel-like material; cartilage reduces friction between the ends of the bones at your joints and cushions your joints

cells the smallest parts of your body; many cells have special jobs to do; for example, a muscle cell is a cell with a special job

colon the first part of your large intestine; it squeezes most of the water out of the wastes left over after digestion

compound machine a machine made up of two or more simple machines

conservation saving or reusing resources so they will be available for the future; for example, turning off the lights when you leave a room conserves energy

D

digestion the process of breaking down food into nutrients for your body to use

E

ecosystem a system formed by the interactions of all the living and non-living things in an environment; an ocean and a forest are both ecosystems

effort force the force that is needed to push, pull, or lift an object

environmental impact the result of an action or event that damages or changes an environment; environmental impacts can be large or small; for example, oil leaking into the ocean can have a large impact on the water organisms

equilibrium the state when the forces acting on an object are balanced; when an object is in equilibrium, the motion of the object does not change

esophagus a long tube that runs from your mouth to your stomach; muscles squeeze food down your esophagus

extract to take something out of something else; for example, ores are extracted from the ground

F

force a push or pull that can change the way an object moves, stop it, or hold it in place

friction a force that resists motion; friction happens when two surfaces come in contact with each other

fulcrum the fixed point on which a lever turns

G

groundwater precipitation that goes into the ground; groundwater that is not brought to the surface will eventually flow into a stream, lake, or river

H

harvesting taking any resource, including water, from Earth's surface

heart an organ that works like a pump; it pushes your blood through your whole body

I

inclined plane a simple machine with a sloped surface like a ramp

Indigenous Knowledge (IK) understandings about the natural world unique to a particular group or culture who have lived for a very long time in that area; this knowledge is passed to the next generation through stories and songs

K

kidneys organs that filter blood; they filter out the wastes and return nutrients and most of the water back to the blood

L

large intestine a wide, short tube connected to your small intestine; it gets rid of the wastes in your body that are left over after digestion

leaching the process of carrying substances such as chemicals into the ground with groundwater

lever a simple machine with a straight rod or board that turns around a fixed point

ligaments strong, elastic groups of cells that stretch and tighten, like rubber bands; they hold the bones of movable joints together

liver an organ that helps break down the fats in food by putting chemical juices into your small intestine

load the weight of an object that is being moved

local environment all the living and non-living things in a particular area

lung a spongy organ in your chest that sits inside your ribs; your blood picks up oxygen and gives up carbon dioxide in your two lungs

M

membrane the outer part of a cell that lets needed materials enter the cell and lets wastes move out of the cell

muscles tissues attached to bones; muscles make bones move

N

natural resources all the living and non-living materials in nature, such as plants, animals, water, wind, and minerals

nerve cells specialized cells that receive messages and then send the messages to other nerve cells

nerves bundles of nerve cells; messages are received and sent from nerve cell to nerve cell along a nerve; nerves send these messages to and from the brain or the spinal cord

non-renewable cannot reproduce or renew itself; once non-renewable resources are used, they are gone forever

nutrients materials that your body needs to stay alive and grow; digestion changes the food you eat into nutrients

O

organ any part that carries out special jobs in your body; organs work together in systems, for example, your stomach is an organ that is part of your digestive system

oxygen a gas found in the air you breathe in; oxygen releases the energy from the nutrients in your body cells

P

pulley a simple machine that has a rope or chain wrapped around a grooved wheel; there are three types of pulleys: a fixed pulley, a movable pulley, and a combined pulley

pulse a regular beat produced when your heart contracts; you can feel your pulse in your wrist

R

ramp a sloped surface; a surface on an angle

raw materials resources before they are turned into products humans use; for example, trees are raw materials for lumber and pulp and paper

recycling processing a product so it can be used again; for example, aluminum cans may be recycled to make new aluminum cans

reflex an immediate and automatic body response to a message; the message goes only to your spinal cord, not to your brain

renewable can replace itself through reproduction, be re-grown, or can renew itself naturally; can be living or non-living

resources any living or non-living things that humans use to meet their needs and wants

S

screw a simple machine that has an inclined plane wrapped around a central core to form a spiral

sense organs parts that gather information from outside your body and send the information to your brain through nerves; sense organs include your skin, nose, tongue, eyes, and ears

simple machines the six machines used to make all other machines: the lever, wheel and axle, pulley, inclined plane, wedge, and screw

skin the largest organ in your body; it covers and protects your body and holds all your systems safely inside

small intestine a long, thin winding tube connected to your stomach; it finishes the job of breaking food down into nutrients

soil pollution the state of soil that has been made unclean by chemicals and other harmful substances

solar energy energy that comes from the Sun; solar energy can be changed into heat or electricity

spinal cord a long rod made of many nerves attached to the base of your brain and running down almost to the end of your spinal column; nerves from your body are attached to the spinal cord

stomach a pear-shaped organ at the end of the esophagus; your stomach mixes up food and breaks it down into a watery liquid

surface runoff precipitation that runs along the surface of the land until it flows into a stream, river, lake, or ocean

surface texture the way an object feels, for example, smooth, rough, or slippery

T

tendons strong, elastic groups of cells that stretch and tighten, like rubber bands; they attach muscles to bones

trachea a tube from your throat to your lungs; air travels down your trachea to your lungs, and carbon dioxide travels up out of your lungs

U

unbalanced forces two forces of unequal strength that are acting in opposite directions on an object

V

veins blood vessels that carry blood back to the heart; this blood usually carries carbon dioxide

W

water cycle the natural recycling of water on Earth so it can be used over and over again; water recycles through evaporation, condensation, and precipitation

water pollution the state of water that has been made unclean by harmful substances or organisms that can make animals and plants sick

watershed an area of land that drains into a river or lake; precipitation that falls on a watershed either flows down to the river or lake, or sinks into the ground

wedge a simple machine with a thick end and a thin end; the thin end is used to lift, hold, or push objects apart

weight a measure of the force of gravity on an object; weight is measured in newtons (N)

wheel a circular object, the larger part of a wheel and axle (a simple machine) that turns around a rod

work the result of using force to make something move

Index

N

Nail guns, 67
Nails, 130
Natural gas, 225–26
Natural resources, 161, 162
Nerve cells, 139, 142
Nerves, 139, 140, 141, 148, 151
Nervous system, 65, 138
   interaction with other
      systems, 150–51
   parts of, 139–41
   role-playing, 154–55
Newtons (N), 8
N'ha'a'itk, 74–75
Nisga'a fish wheels, 76–77
Non-living resources, 162, 178
Non-living things, 161, 162, 165,
   166, 167, 216
Non-renewable resources, 159,
   204–207, 227, 230–31
Nose, 92, 93, 141, 148
Nutrients, 88, 89, 92, 99, 101,
   105, 107, 119

O

Ocean, 226
Offshore rigs, 226
Ogopogo, 74–75
Oil, 225–26, 227
Ores, 208, 209, 210, 214–15
Organs, 87, 88, 119, 132, 150
Oxygen, 92, 93, 94, 101, 103,
   104, 105, 106, 107

P

Packaging, 169
Pancreas, 89
Peat, 206
Pencil sharpeners, 34, 53
Pencils, 24, 25, 208
Petroleum, 163
Phosphates, 194
Plants, 212–13
Plasma, 106, 107
Plastics, 213
Platelets, 106
Ploughs, 66
Pollutants, 192, 193, 210, 225

Pollution, 212, 213, 222. *See also*
   Air pollution; Soil pollution;
   Water pollution
Polyester, 163
Power boats, 66
Precipitation, 191
Products
   copper, 215
   forestry, 186-87
Propellers, 53
Pulleys, 36–37, 45–47
   combined, 46
   fixed, 45, 46, 62
   inclined planes and, 63
   in mining machines, 69
   movable, 46
   in sawmills, 73
Pulp and paper products,
   186–87
Pulse, 102, 108

R

Ramps, 15, 17–18, 20–23, 48
Raw materials, 186, 215
Reaction time, 146–47
Reclamation, 217
Rectum, 89
Recycling, 170, 191, 214
Reducing, 169
Reflex actions, 144
Reflexes, 144–45
Renewable resources, 159,
   176–79, 178, 198–99, 202–203
Resources. *See also* Non-
   renewable resources;
   Renewable resources
   conservation of, 168–71
   and environment, 160
   impact of use, 164–66
   processing of, 182
   recycling, 170
   reducing use of, 169
   reusing, 170
   use of, 232–33
Respiratory system, 92–95, 133
Reusing, 170
Ribs, 95, 121, 123
Robotic arms, 64, 65, 129

Robots, 64–65
Rocks, 208, 210, 214, 217
Roller coasters, 3, 23
Rollers, 42
Ruminating, 91

S

Saliva, 89
Salmon, 180–83
Salt water, 191
Sawmills, 73
Scissors, 60
Screws, 36–37, 52–53
   on bicycles, 61
   on can openers, 60
   on scissors, 60
Sense organs, 140, 141, 148–49,
   151
Senses, 148–49
Shovels, 59, 68
Sight, 148
Simple machines, 32, 36–38, 58,
   74–75
Skateboarding, 4
Skeleton, 119, 132
Skin, 118, 130–31, 132, 133, 141,
   148
Skull, 120, 122, 131, 139
Slope
   force and, 17–18
   rolling and, 20–23
Small intestine, 89
Smell, 148
Smoking, 99
Snakes, 91
Snowboarding, 4
Snow person, 33
Soaps, 195
Soccer, 5, 6
Soil pollution, 192, 212–13
Solar energy, 199
Sound, 149
Spinal column, 120, 123, 140
Spinal cord, 139, 140, 141
Spirals, 52, 53
Spring scales, 8, 9
Stomach, 87, 89, 91, 151
Sun, the, 178, 199

Credits

GLENMORE ELEMENTARY
960 Glenmore Drive
Kelowna, B.C.
V1Y 4P1

GLENMORE ELEMENTARY
960 Glenmore Drive
Kelowna, B.C.
V1Y 4P1